"For evangelicals and Protestants wanting to know what theology is and hungering for mystery and liturgy and sacrament in the historical church, this is a beautifully written guide to going further up and further in."

—**Gerald R. McDermott**, Beeson Divinity School, Samford University (retired); author of *Everyday Glory*

"Clark and Johnson helpfully remind us that theology matters not because we need to fill our heads with abstract philosophical ideas but because it is our way of responding to the reality of the triune God, who has called us to enter into his life and purposes. Let this volume take you back to the heart of the formative nature of true theology—fostering our worship of God and letting his reality re-shape us in his goodness and truth."

—**Kelly M. Kapic**, Covenant College

"If the church is to succeed in forming people who look like Jesus, it will need a theology that is up to the task. In this wonderful introduction, Clark and Johnson show us that theology is not the dusty domain of academic specialists but real, saving, and transforming knowledge of the living God given by Christ to his church for a purpose: the edification and maturity of God's people into the image of Christ."

—**Joel Scandrett**, Trinity School for Ministry; editor of *To Be a Christian: An Anglican Catechism*

"This presentation of the foundational role of orthodox, biblical theology in daily life and work will be of great encouragement to students and pastors, as well as lay persons who are serious about building their lives on the unshakeable foundation laid down by the Word of God in Jesus Christ. I admire the authors' forthright affirmation of the concrete, life-giving nature of theological study, graciously expounded here for the well-being of the church and for the daily lives of serious disciples of Jesus. He is honored here as the

Savior and Lord of the mind as well as the bodily life and destiny of all who seek him."

—**Fleming Rutledge**, author of *The Crucifixion: Understanding the Death of Jesus Christ*

"This wonderful book offers a clarion call to make the knowledge of God the most important thing in our lives, the thing we long for, delight in, pursue, and prioritize above all else—and use to interpret and apply everything else in our lives as well. It offers a call, in other words, to recover the significance of theology once again in an age when most Christians pay lip service to God without knowing much about him. May real, genuine growth in our knowledge of the Lord renew our minds, shape our thoughts, and fuel our lives."

—**Douglas A. Sweeney**, Beeson Divinity School, Samford University

"Being called to formation means nothing less than being called to Christ. That's the basic premise of *A Call to Christian Formation*. From start to finish, this book invites us to share in the mind of Christ. Bold and unapologetic, Clark and Johnson ward off all wanderlust—away from God in Christ, away from the church and her liturgy, away from mystery and paradox. Grounded in Scripture and conversant with ecumenical thought, this book powerfully reminds us that the Christ-reality is the only place where true communion is found."

—**Hans Boersma**, Nashotah House Theological Seminary

A CALL TO CHRISTIAN FORMATION

A CALL TO CHRISTIAN FORMATION

HOW THEOLOGY MAKES SENSE OF OUR WORLD

JOHN C. CLARK
AND MARCUS PETER JOHNSON

Baker Academic
a division of Baker Publishing Group
Grand Rapids, Michigan

Published by Baker Academic
a division of Baker Publishing Group
PO Box 6287, Grand Rapids, MI 49516-6287
www.bakeracademic.com

Printed in the United States of America

Library of Congress Cataloging-in-Publication Data
Names: Clark, John C., 1970– author. | Johnson, Marcus Peter, 1971– author.
Title: A call to Christian formation : how theology makes sense of our world / John C.
    Clark and Marcus Peter Johnson.
Description: Grand Rapids, Michigan : Baker Academic, a division of Baker Publishing
    Group, 2021. | Includes index.
Identifiers: LCCN 2020051887 | ISBN 9781540960689 (paperback) | ISBN
    9781540964243 (casebound)
Subjects: LCSH: Theology. | Theology, Doctrinal. | Christian philosophy.
Classification: LCC BR118 .C48 2021 | DDC 230—dc23
LC record available at https://lccn.loc.gov/2020051887

Scripture quotations are from The Holy Bible, English Standard Version® (ESV®), copyright © 2001 by Crossway, a publishing ministry of Good News Publishers. Used by permission. All rights reserved. ESV Text Edition: 2016

In keeping with biblical principles of creation stewardship, Baker Publishing Group advocates the responsible use of our natural resources. As a member of the Green Press Initiative, our company uses recycled paper when possible. The text paper of this book is composed in part of post-consumer waste.

21   22   23   24   25   26   27   7   6   5   4   3   2   1

For Victor Shepherd, our blessed *Doktorvater*,
to whom we are eternally grateful.

For our students, our fellow pilgrims,
who make teaching theology a joy.

For the church, the holy body and bride of Jesus,
may this token of our love be of service to you.

Contents

Acknowledgments

Winston Churchill once said, "Writing a book is an adventure. To begin with, it is a toy and an amusement; then it becomes a mistress, and then it becomes a master, and then a tyrant. The last phase is that just as you are about to be reconciled to your servitude, you kill the monster, and fling him out to the public."[1] Just about everyone who has brought a book to completion can relate at some level to Churchill's playful description of what at points is a painful process, and we are certainly no exception. Except rather than flinging a dead thing into the world, we hope to be releasing something that is quite alive—a living, lively, joy-filled offering to the God who is life himself.

Of course, writing a book is no solitary adventure. There is much support along the way, so much gratitude is in order. Many thanks to the entire team at Baker Academic for the skill and kindness exuded at every step and stage of the journey. In particular, thanks to Bob Hosack for championing this project from the start, and for being patient and encouraging to the end; to James Korsmo, for being a

1. Winston S. Churchill, speech at the National Book Exhibition Awards Ceremony, Grosvenor House, London, November 2, 1949, quoted in Martin Gilbert, *Never Despair: 1945–1965*, vol. 8 of *Winston S. Churchill* (Boson: Houghton Mifflin, 1988). I (John) am indebted for this quote to my trusty teaching assistants, Ben and Ireland Mast.

superb editor with a servant's heart; and to Kara Day, Paula Gibson, Sarah Gombis, and Michael Nix-Walkup, for being exceedingly competent and unremittingly pleasant. What is more, how rich we are to have friends the likes of ours. We wish we could name you all here, because we are indeed thankful to and for you. But Bill and Linda MacKillop, Rich and Ann Nikchevich, John and Krista Scheidt, and Matt Woodley—you took especial care to prayerfully walk with us on this adventure; we are now and forever grateful. Praise and thanks be to God for you, one and all. Lastly but mostly, we give thanks to our wives and children. To our beloved brides, Kate Clark and Stacie Johnson, this book would never have been started, not to mention finished, if not for your immense love and support—gentle and strong, faithful and true; thank you. And to our children—William and Gwyneth Clark, and Peter, Abel, and Samuel Johnson—your dads are well aware that our writing is not without cost to you, so please know that we are both grateful and proud. Dear ones, we pray that you make haste in your youth to do the grandest, wisest, most authentically human thing you ever could do: answer the call of Christ to be formed in Christ, the call of which this book speaks.

Abbreviations

ANF	*Ante-Nicene Fathers*. Edited by Alexander Roberts and James Donaldson. 10 vols. Reprint, Peabody, MA: Hendrickson, 1994
BC	*The Book of Concord: The Confessions of the Evangelical Lutheran Church*. Edited by Robert Kolb and Timothy J. Wengert. Translated by Charles Arand et al. Minneapolis: Fortress, 2000
CC	*Creeds of the Churches: A Reader in Christian Doctrine from the Bible to the Present*. 3rd ed. Edited by John H. Leith. Louisville: John Knox, 1982
Inst.	John Calvin. *Institutes of the Christian Religion*. 2 vols. Edited by John T. McNeill. Translated by Ford Lewis Battles. Library of Christian Classics. Philadelphia: Westminster, 1960
LW	Martin Luther. *Luther's Works*. American Edition. 55 vols. Edited by Jaroslav Pelikan and Helmut Lehmann. St. Louis: Concordia; Philadelphia: Fortress, 1955–86
NPNF[1]	*The Nicene and Post-Nicene Fathers*. Series 1. Edited by Philip Schaff. 14 vols. 1886–89. Reprint, Peabody, MA: Hendrickson, 1994
NPNF[2]	*The Nicene and Post-Nicene Fathers*. Series 2. Edited by Philip Schaff and Henry Wace. 14 vols. Reprint, Peabody, MA: Hendrickson, 1994

Introduction

Theology: Formed by Christ the Lord

Christian theology exists in many forms, in many places, and for many types of people. It is practiced both in the halls of academia and in the pews of the church. Theology thrives as a scholarly discipline, and it also flourishes in the songs and prayers of Sunday worship. It can be both sophisticated and simple, every bit as home in the scholar's study as in Sunday school. Thomas Aquinas's erudite tome *Summa Theologiae* is a work of theology, but so is Martin Luther's Small Catechism, published for Christian parents to train their children. The reason theology can exist in so many forms and places, and across a spectrum of diverse understanding, is that theology is dedicated, above all else, to knowledge of God. J. I. Packer gives the very best justification for the study of theology: "What were we made for? To know God. What aim should we set ourselves in life? To know God. What is the 'eternal life' that Jesus gives? Knowledge of God. 'This is eternal life: that they may know you, the only true God, and Jesus Christ, whom you have sent' (John 17:3). What is the best thing in life, bringing more joy, delight and contentment than anything else? Knowledge of God. . . . What, of all the states God ever sees man in, gives God most pleasure?

Knowledge of himself."[1] Our Lord Jesus himself instructs his followers, "Love the Lord your God with all your heart and with all your soul and with all your mind" (Matt. 22:37). Loving God with our minds, no less than with our hearts and souls, is a holy commission and calling for every last disciple of Christ. To know God is to love him, and to love God is to know him. And it is precisely in this context of knowing and loving God that theology has its proper place—for if theology ever ceases to be preoccupied with a passionate knowledge of God, then theology ceases to be truly what it is.

Theology can be defined in several ways. It can, of course, be defined as "the study or science of God." This definition is serviceable so far as it goes, yet it lacks the verve, vitality, and specificity required for Christian formation. What we are after is a definition of *theology* that is richly and robustly Christian, a definition that unapologetically owns the fact that the triune God of the gospel is truly known in Jesus Christ. Therefore, we think it is far better to seek an overtly biblical basis for a definition of *theology*, a basis found in John 1:1. There we find two Greek terms, *theos* and *logos*, used in the closest proximity. "In the beginning was the Word [*logos*], and the Word was with God [*theos*], and the Word was God." *Theology*, put in straightforward biblical terms, simply means "word about God," or "God-word." And as we clearly see in Scripture, that unique and definitive "word about God" was and is the eternal Son and Word of God, Jesus Christ. All truly *Christ-ian* theology, therefore, is defined by the *Theos-Logos*, the God in Word. That Word of God has become flesh, incarnating the revelation of God to humanity. Theology, then, properly and literally speaking, concerns knowledge of God revealed in and through the incarnate Christ. Theology must be preoccupied with an appropriately faithful response to this revelation, lest it cease to be what theology truly is.

To be even more precise, we can say that theology is *the deliberate and considered response by the people of God to the revelation*

1. J. I. Packer, *Knowing God*, 20th anniv. ed. (Downers Grove, IL: InterVarsity, 1993), 33.

of God in Christ, where we offer joyful and worshipful expression to the truth and the reality found in him. Theology exists because God has spoken, and his Word is worth living and hoping in. And theology seeks to express that life and hope in all that we think, believe, feel, pray, and sing. Indeed, if one were to say what Christian theology does in its most basic form, it would be that theology helps the church to sing to Jesus Christ.[2] To say it another way, theology involves the reordering of our minds and hearts—our reasoning and our desiring—to God as he is revealed and embodied in Jesus Christ. In union with Christ, and by the power of the Holy Spirit, all of our assumptions about the nature of reality are confronted, challenged, and brought into conformity with the strange and wonderful reality of God, which sets our minds and hearts free to know and love the Truth.[3] Theology, then, is the science and art of succumbing to the sacred impress of Christ on our lives, so that instead of being conformed to the world, we may be "transformed by the renewal of [our] mind[s]" (Rom. 12:2).

C. S. Lewis famously provoked us to take honest assessment of the place of Jesus Christ in our lives. Wishing to prevent any and all cynical, superficial, or moralistic evasions of the issue, Lewis laid down the gauntlet, the trilemma, in fact. Jesus is a lunatic, a liar, or our Lord. Lewis's comments are highly instructive and entirely relevant for the purpose and goal of theology:

> I am trying here to prevent anyone saying the really foolish thing that people often say about Him: "I'm ready to accept Jesus as a great moral teacher, but I don't accept His claim to be God." That is the

---

2. Stanley J. Grenz and Roger E. Olson offer a commendable definition of theology: "Christian theology is reflecting on and articulating the God-centered life and beliefs that Christians share as followers of Jesus Christ, and it is done in order that God may be glorified in all Christians are and do. *Soli Deo gloria.*" *Who Needs Theology? An Invitation to the Study of God* (Downers Grove, IL: InterVarsity, 1996), 49.

3. Alan E. Lewis, *Between Cross and Resurrection: A Theology of Holy Saturday* (Grand Rapids: Eerdmans, 2001), 136.

one thing we must not say. A man who was merely a man and said the sort of things Jesus said would not be a great moral teacher. He would either be a lunatic—on the level with the man who says he is a poached egg—or else he would be the Devil of Hell. You must make your choice. Either this man was, and is, the Son of God: or else a madman or something worse. You can shut Him up for a fool, you can spit at Him and kill Him as a demon; or you can fall at His feet and call Him Lord and God. But let us not come with any patronizing nonsense about His being a great human teacher. He has not left that open to us. He did not intend to.[4]

According to Lewis, we do not have the option of treating Jesus as a dispenser of enlightened moral teachings. Jesus does not need to be Lord of heaven and earth to do that. If he is Lord, then he is certainly Lord of our hearts, souls, and minds. And so we cannot, indeed we must not, pay lip service to our Lord without offering the whole of who we are to the whole of who he is. We have been re-created in Christ Jesus to be transformed into his resplendent image, and while that transformation surely involves more than theological formation, it just as surely involves no less. We were made to have our minds and hearts conformed to and transformed by the loving lordship of Jesus. And that is what theology is all about: the liberating conformity of our whole persons to the truth of the all-encompassing reality of God.

This book seeks to recover and warmly commend the ancient claim that theology is the fountain of all true knowledge, that theology, because it seeks to know and express the truth of God, shapes and determines how we understand reality—even as it brings us into conformity with that reality. In a world where claims about truth are increasingly suspect, such a claim may seem extravagant. And so, as Robert Jenson notes, "We may press theology's claim very bluntly by noting that theology, with whatever sophistication or lack thereof,

---

4. C. S. Lewis, *Mere Christianity*, rev. and exp. ed. (New York: HarperOne, 2015), 52.

claims to know the one God of all and so to know the one decisive fact about all things, so that theology must be either a universal and founding discipline or a delusion."[5] Jenson's argument is elegant and exactly right. If theology claims to know God, who is himself the foundation of all human knowledge, then theology is either fundamental or fraudulent. If reality does *not* reside in knowledge of the God of truth, then reality can, *and indeed must*, be found elsewhere. Conversely, if God is the source and ground of all truth, then truth can, indeed must, be found nowhere else than in God, the ground and context of all human knowing. Either way, nothing less or other than reality hangs in the balance.

That knowledge of God is a priority for the apprehension of reality appears at first glance a simple truism for Christians. Who would seriously deny it? Yet theology, which is dedicated to the knowledge, love, and enjoyment of God, is increasingly viewed in negative terms by many in the church. Keith Johnson notes the apparent contradiction: "Given its noble purpose, its prominent place in church history and the real contributions it makes to the church's contemporary life, one would think that the discipline of theology has a positive reputation among Christians—but it does not. . . . In fact, many smart and faithful Christians cringe when they hear the word *theology* due to the negative connotations the discipline carries. Some even reject the very idea of theology and insist that they can live faithfully without it simply trusting God and believing the words of Scripture."[6] Despite its historical pedigree and present promise, theology has lost its place among many Christians who would otherwise be happy to affirm that knowledge of God is the foundation of truth and reality. What accounts for this sad state of affairs? How do we explain the current malaise in the church regarding theology?

---

5. Robert W. Jenson, *Systematic Theology*, vol. 1, *The Triune God* (New York: Oxford University Press, 1997), 20.

6. Keith L. Johnson, *Theology as Discipleship* (Downers Grove, IL: IVP Academic, 2015), 20 (emphasis original).

The Demise of Theology

Theology was once considered the basis of authentic human knowledge. In a phrase frequently attributed to Thomas Aquinas, theology was hailed as the "queen of the sciences." John Calvin echoed Aquinas when he wrote, "Knowledge of all the sciences is mere smoke, where the heavenly science of Christ is wanting. . . . In other respects, too, it holds true, that without Christ sciences in every department are vain, and that the man who knows not God is vain, though he should be conversant with every branch of learning."[7] Given what past intellectual luminaries like Aquinas and Calvin urged about the importance of theology, it seems an understatement to say that theology does not occupy the same place for most modern intellectuals. For instance, H. L. Mencken (1880–1956), the esteemed journalist, author, and pundit of American Christianity, once defined *theology* thus: "Theology—An effort to explain the unknowable by putting it into terms of the not worth knowing."[8] Even if we recognize that Mencken's sentiment came from someone largely sympathetic to the Christian faith, it would not be long before such assertions became far more acerbic. Indeed, the renowned Oxford evolutionary biologist Richard Dawkins has been brash enough, in our own time, to dismiss theology altogether:

> What has theology ever said that is the smallest use to anybody? When has theology ever said anything that is demonstrably true and is not obvious? I have listened to theologians, read them, debated against them. I have never heard any of them ever say anything of the smallest use, anything that was not either platitudinously obvious or downright false. If all the achievements of scientists were wiped out tomorrow, there would be no doctors but witch doctors, no transport

7. John Calvin, *Calvin's Commentaries*, Calvin Translation Society (Edinburgh, 1844–56; reprinted in 22 vols., Grand Rapids: Baker Books, 2003), 20:82–83, on 1 Cor. 1:20.

8. H. L. Mencken, "*Arcana Coelestia*," in *A Mencken Chrestomathy* (1949; repr., New York: Knopf, 1967), 624.

faster than horses, no computers, no printed books, no agriculture beyond subsistence peasant farming. If all the achievements of theologians were wiped out tomorrow, would anyone notice the smallest difference? Even the bad achievements of scientists, the bombs, and sonar-guided whaling vessels work! The achievements of theologians don't do anything, don't affect anything, don't mean anything. What makes anyone think that "theology" is a subject at all?[9]

As a measure of the hard times on which theology has fallen, it is sometimes difficult to say whether contemporary Christians resonate more with the assertions of Aquinas and Calvin or Mencken—or perhaps even Dawkins. Certainly, Dawkins's histrionic screed invites criticism for a number of reasons. Aside from peddling the denatured science of scientism and prizing utilitarian pragmatism in such a way as to eclipse all other considerations, he is inartful, wildly overblown, and nearly hysterical in tone. Still, the perception persists that theology is too often pedantic and obscure, fit more for ridicule than riveted attention. Sadly, for many in the church the conviction that theology is the *regina artium* ("queen of the sciences") can sound either quaintly nostalgic or hopelessly idealistic.

Understood in a broader perspective, there has been a seismic, architectonic shift in the way people think about how knowledge is gained and secured, especially since the dawn of the Enlightenment. A host of forces—intellectual, cultural, psychological, technological, political, and ideological—have pushed theology to the margins. And the church is not immune. Suffice it to say, theology can hardly flourish with the assumption, explicit or implicit, that the quest for knowledge is hindered by the introduction of theological claims. And whether we Christians are altogether cognizant of this revolution in the nature of knowledge, it is still the epistemological stream in which we swim. The way most people thought about truth and knowledge before the Enlightenment assumed a theocentric universe, one in

---

9. Richard Dawkins, "The Emptiness of Theology," *Free Inquiry* 18, no. 2 (Spring 1998): 6.

which a transcendent being governed the facts of life. The underlying truth that defined the way people thought about heaven and earth was substantiated by reference to divine revelation. In its specific Western form, this meant reliance on a Judeo-Christian understanding of the world. No wonder theology had pride of place among Christians who sought to know reality; God simply *was* that reality.

The epistemological movement of the Enlightenment was a tidal change, the alteration of an orbit. It rested on a different basis altogether: that knowledge of reality was obtained and secured from within human cognition, quite apart from divine revelation. Indeed, revelation came to be perceived as a hindrance in the quest for authentic human knowledge. In this new, modern paradigm, true knowledge rests on a scientific method liberated from the constraints of theological pronouncements or epiphanies. Immanuel Kant (1724–1804), one of the most influential champions of this new paradigm, described it like this: "*Enlightenment is the human being's emancipation from its self-incurred immaturity. Immaturity* is the inability to make use of one's intellect without the direction of another. This immaturity is *self-incurred* when its cause does not lie in a lack of intellect, but rather in a lack of resolve and courage to make use of one's intellect without the direction of another. '*Sapere aude!* Have the courage to make use of your own intellect!' is hence the motto of enlightenment."[10] Kant's motto signals, in effect, that the controlling center that determined reality moved from divine revelation in concert with human cognition to human cognition absent any authority outside itself. Science (knowledge) became increasingly insular and self-referential, beholden to nothing but its own internal tests of logic. To critique the epistemological sea change that is the Enlightenment is not to deny that some extraordinary scientific advances have come in its wake—or that many of those advances came from people of profound Christian faith. But

10. Immanuel Kant, "An Answer to the Question: What Is Enlightenment?," in *"Toward Perpetual Peace" and Other Writings on Politics, Peace, and History*, ed. Pauline Kleingeld, trans. David L. Colclasure (New Haven: Yale University Press, 2006), 17 (emphasis original).

it is to suggest, with Kelly Kapic, that a good bit of the Enlightenment "was a mirage, and an undesirable one at that."[11]

However we may judge this revolution in scientific knowledge, the words of Louis Dupré are arresting: "Theology lost its hold on a culture whose substance it had once shaped. It became reduced to a science among others, with a method and object exclusively its own. Other sciences henceforth could freely ignore it."[12] Of course, ignorance of theology can happen in more than one way. Theology can be outright dismissed, as is often the case among modern intellectuals. But theology can also be more subtly ignored with the ostensible design of accommodating it. Under the guise of concern and admiration for theology, it can be conscripted for other purposes, put to other ends, with the inevitable result that it loses its identity and authority. In this latter case, theology is often used to provide the sanction of divine authority even as it is subsumed under the auspices of other fields of knowledge. Theology can then run the risk of becoming a cipher—absorbed, as Richard John Neuhaus notes, by alternate realities:

> In relating Christianity to some other way of constructing reality, the other way too often demonstrates the greater power of absorption. The result, from the Christian viewpoint, is apostasy. To be sure, that is not the intention, but here as elsewhere intentions may have little to do with consequences.
>
> Thus we must view with robust skepticism the proposition that good sociology, or psychology, is good theology, and vice versa. One suspects that those who say such things have a stronger idea of what good sociology (or psychology) is than they do of what good theology is. The reason for this is not to be found in a moral fault but in the very structure of intellectual discourse in our world.[13]

---

11. Kelly M. Kapic, *A Little Book for New Theologians: Why and How to Study Theology* (Downers Grove, IL: IVP Academic, 2012), 41n1.

12. Louis Dupré, *Passage to Modernity: An Essay in the Hermeneutics of Nature and Culture* (New Haven: Yale University Press, 1993), 189.

13. Richard John Neuhaus, *Freedom for Ministry*, rev. ed. (Grand Rapids: Eerdmans, 1992), 146.

Whether by outright rejection or through absorption, the place of theology in modern discourse has become marginalized, both explicitly and implicitly. If the supremacy of divine revelation is denied, after all, the quest for understanding reality must be located elsewhere.

The church must resist the temptation to believe that other types of knowledge are capable of grounding, verifying, or legitimating knowledge of the Lord and his specific call to submit *all* of our lives to his glorious and all-encompassing revelation of reality. For the church to be free to proclaim that God has revealed the meaning of heaven and earth in Jesus Christ, theology must be free to exercise its own intellectual domain, free—but never disengaged—from the structure of discourse in our world. The church must always be alert to the misguided assumption that the Word of God is beholden to humanity's self-appointed, and deified, notions of the authority of universal reason—an assumption that will not recognize Christ as the Lord of the truth, which he alone can define and determine. Murray Rae forcefully asserts that theology cannot be based on any other authority: "If God is the Triune God, revealed in Jesus Christ through the power of the Spirit, and testified to in Scripture, then theology is not predicated upon any human capacity or mode of thinking, but upon the initiative of God in making himself known to us and reconciling the world to himself."[14] Either Jesus Christ is Lord or he is not. And if he is indeed Lord, then he is certainly the Lord of how we understand truth and reality.

The Recovery of Theology

If it is true that Christians no longer regard theology as having pride of place in the human quest for knowledge, then the overarching theme of this book—*our theological beliefs shape and determine our under-*

14. Murray Rae, "Prolegomena," in *Trinitarian Soundings in Systematic Theology*, ed. Paul Louis Metzger (London: T&T Clark, 2006), 9–10.

standing of reality—appears outlandish. How can a conviction like this be sustained among Christians for whom the study of theology has become marginalized, if not neglected or ignored? The burden of this book is to demonstrate the essential role theology plays in the way Christians understand the deepest truths of human existence and meaning. To cite Calvin once again, "Nearly all the wisdom we possess, that is to say, true and sound wisdom, consists of two parts: the knowledge of God and of ourselves."[15] That order is not arbitrary, as Calvin knew well. For unless we *first* truly know God, we cannot truly know ourselves or the rest of creation. If Christians have lost this all-encompassing sense of the priority of the knowledge of God with respect to every other kind of knowledge, it is high time to recover it. If Christians really do believe that God is the fundamental ground of all truth and meaning—which all do, in theory at least—it is time to recapture the grand and glorious heart of that conviction.

What we take most joy *in*, we are most preoccupied *with*. This applies to theology above all else, due to its exalted subject. Knowledge of God is the supreme aim and end of human existence, the deepest joy we can experience. And theology is nothing other than the articulation of that joy-filled goal in word, thought, prayer, and song. What will it require, then, for the church to recover a deep sense of the importance of theology for our understanding of reality? A renewed love affair with God, above all else. It will require a steady and resolved determination to have our minds and hearts seized by the singular beauty of Christ Jesus. It will depend on a steadfast conviction that Jesus Christ is the Alpha and Omega of all reality, Lord and King of all other would-be lords and kings. It will demand submission to the sublime truth that Jesus is the Way, and the Truth, and the Life of both God and humanity. If theology will once again resume its proper place as the "queen of the sciences," which God alone can provide, it will surely involve the following kinds of affirmations, convictions, and commitments among Christians.

---

15. John Calvin, *Inst.* 1.1.1.

First, an acknowledgment that theology can never mean anything less or other than cheerful obedience to the command of Jesus Christ: "You shall love the Lord your God with all your heart and with all your soul and with all your mind" (Matt. 22:37; cf. Luke 10:27; Mark 12:30–31). This sentence is so familiar to most Christians that it may not strike us as the lodestar that it is for the privilege of doing theology. But in fact, there is hardly a better way of thinking about what theology is: devoted attention in heart, soul, and mind to loving God. This whole-person devotion leads us to pursue God in all that he is with all that we are. Christian formation involves more than theology, but certainly not less. The Lord calls us to a loving reorientation of our hearts, minds, and souls to the Truth that he is. And so, even if theology is neither the totality of Christian formation nor a substitute for that formation, theology remains indispensable to it. With heart, soul, and mind we "take every thought captive to obey Christ" (2 Cor. 10:5).

Second, a recovery of theology in the life of the church will involve an abiding commitment to Holy Scripture. Whenever and wherever the church has been theologically alive and alert, it has been because Christians have nurtured a love affair with the Bible. Properly understood and faithfully practiced, theology is enamored of the Word of God, proclaimed and written by the prophets and apostles of God, and inspired by the very Spirit of God. The gospel of our Lord Jesus is the focal point of theology. And as Dietrich Bonhoeffer wrote so wisely: "Nothing is more important for the student of theology than to inquire more and more carefully, more and more objectively, more and more openly, more and more in love, concerning the truth of the gospel."[16] A renaissance of theology will go hand in hand with a renaissance of deep-seated love for, and devoted attention to, Holy Scripture. The same as it ever was.

Third, a recovery of theology will require the frank and humble admission that our human apprehension of reality—the very course

16. Dietrich Bonhoeffer, "Becoming Real Theologians," in *The Trials of Theology: Becoming a 'Proven Worker' in a Dangerous Business*, ed. Andrew J. B. Cameron and Brian S. Rosner (Fearn, Ross-shire, UK: Christian Focus, 2010), 73.

of our thinking and the structures that underlie human reason—has been seriously compromised and damaged by our fall into sin. The human intellect, in other words, has suffered the effects of sin no less than the rest of our human capacities. We are sinners in heart, soul, body, and mind—and sinful people think sinfully! Therefore, it is not obvious to us how to conceive of reality unless we be converted to the truth. The task of theology requires a reorientation of our fallen hearts and minds to a reality that we cannot earn or achieve in our own strength. Our ability to discern and desire reality needs to undergo the sanctifying effect of participation in the death and resurrection of the Lord Jesus. Truthful comprehension of reality is not a given for us human beings—it is *learned* through dying and rising with Jesus. "Theology, therefore, is a form of participation in the new life made possible in and through Christ, a new life in which our thinking and speaking is transformed so that we no longer think in terms of *what seems theologically real and true to us* but in terms of what has been accomplished by God in Christ."[17] What is true for every other aspect of Christian formation is no less true for theology: it too must undergo the mortification and vivification that comes from union with Christ. John Webster rightly insists: "Theological reason thus shares in the baptismal pattern of all aspects of Christian existence. Caught up by the Holy Spirit into the reconciling work of God in Christ, reason is condemned and redeemed, torn away from its evil attachment to falsehood, vanity and dissipation, and so cleansed and sanctified for service in the knowledge of the truth of the gospel."[18] It is crucial to grasp that theology requires neither the abandonment nor the diminishment of reason and rationality but rather their reconstruction in accordance with the rationality of God. Theology involves the "conversion of the mind to God's own reasoning (cf. Rom. 12:2), the fresh examination of previously fixed conceptions in obedience to the

---

17. Rae, "Prolegomena," 15 (emphasis added).
18. John Webster, *Confessing God: Essays in Christian Dogmatics II* (London: T&T Clark, 2005), 4.

word that has been heard, mental surrender to the sheer force of the story listened to."[19]

Whenever sane and sober, Christian theology is prefaced by the jarring confession that our human understanding of reality is *not* self-explanatory. In other words, so far from being the datum point and controlling principle for interpreting the world or determining the existence/identity of God, we are not even the datum point and controlling principle for understanding ourselves. Not only do we need God to reveal *God* to us; we need God to reveal *us* to us! Christian theology maintains that knowledge of God is always and ever conditioned by God himself and thus never conditioned by our own self-analysis or self-projection. Basic to God being God is that the living, speaking, triune God of the gospel is *alone* the Lord of his own self-disclosure. Hilary of Poitiers made this point some seventeen centuries ago: "Since . . . we are to discourse of the things of God, let us assume that God has full knowledge of Himself, and bow with humble reverence to His words. For He Whom we can only know through His own utterances is the fitting witness concerning Himself."[20]

Fourth, the recovery of theology necessitates that it be reclaimed as the specific province and mission of the church. The church has a divine calling to proclaim the truth of our Lord Jesus Christ, the Word and gospel of God. Its mission is an unabashedly and unequivocally theological one. "Go therefore and make disciples of all nations, . . . teaching them to observe all that I have commanded you" (Matt. 28:19–20). This Great Commission is more than a call to theological formation, but it can never be less. The church must avoid at all costs turning the Great Commission into a great omission,

19. Lewis, *Between Cross and Resurrection*, 135–36. He then adds: "Rationality and doctrine are not alternatives to, or evasions of, the church's missionary task but the essential preconditions for doing that task. Without cognitive concepts and their rational ordering the People of God could expound neither to themselves nor to others the meaning of what they had seen, heard, and believed" (136).

20. Hilary of Poitiers, *On the Trinity* 1.18, in NPNF[2], 9:45.

where we fail to articulate the beautiful and bracing glory of our Lord Jesus in all of its dimensions. We must reject out of hand the ripping and rending of theology from the life, worship, and mission of the church—as if theology could be delegated to the scholar and relegated to the margins of the church and beyond. Theology's primary and principal aim is to give true expression to the identity and acts of God, and that expression is enacted in the church's worship and witness to the Lord.[21] The student of theology must never succumb to the temptation to sit above the faith of the church in dispassionate detachment, exacerbating the suspicion that theology is a threat to the church rather than its sworn ally.[22] The purpose of theology is to articulate the joy of the gospel, not convolute it; to express the wonder of God, not obscure it. Theological erudition can be a sublime gift to the church, but it must always be put in service to the church's primary mission to rejoice in the Lord, to enjoy intimacy with him, and to proclaim his magnificent name. Hans Boersma punctuates this point: "Theology is not primarily about words; it is about realities. Theology doesn't thrive in a context where the relationship with God is explained primarily as external or nominal; theology as discipline requires an environment in which we experience the relationship with God as participatory and real. Theology is a sacramental discipline: it is an initiation in which our ordinary created existence is taken up into the truth, goodness, and

21. Dubious, then, is the rather recent trend to differentiate doctrine from practice, or as is often expressed in the curriculum of colleges and seminaries, to differentiate dogmatic and systematic theology from practical and pastoral theology. This juxtaposition is contrived and arbitrary, but telling nonetheless. For when theology ceases to be practical and pastoral, it is because it has first ceased to be *theological*. In other words, theology is practical and pastoral precisely *because* it is theological. Theology is about knowledge of God, and nothing is more impractical and nonpastoral than not knowing God. See John C. Clark and Marcus Peter Johnson, *The Incarnation of God: The Mystery of the Gospel as the Foundation of Evangelical Theology* (Wheaton: Crossway, 2015), 40.

22. Confronting this temptation is a fundamental concern of Helmut Thielicke's exquisite introduction to the study of theology, *A Little Exercise for Young Theologians*, trans. Charles L. Taylor (1962; repr., Grand Rapids: Eerdmans, 1998).

beauty of the eternal Word of God and thus participates by grace in the triune life of God."[23]

Charting Our Course

When the church sacrifices or ignores her God-given right and privilege to say true things about the way things truly are, the church becomes impoverished, anemic, weak, and unsteady. Ignorance of and indifference to theology can do nothing else but render Christians clueless, defenseless, and useless. Conversely, when the church embraces her God-given office to say true things about the way things truly are, the church becomes fortified, resilient, strong, and steadfast—winsome and cheerfully confident to express reality as it really is. The benefits for the church are innumerable, but so too for the world. One of the gifts of service and love the church gives to the world through Christ, in fact, is the truth.

This does not mean that theological expression will be uncontroversial or uncontested. East of Eden, that is quite impossible. Because theology deals with the very deepest matters of human existence, it makes a claim on our lives that is bound to be disturbing. Yet, according to John Webster, "theology is and *ought* to be disturbing, for at its heart lie those events in which, according to Christian faith, human life and thought are entirely transfigured."[24] The student of theology must be ever aware that claims about ultimate reality are not likely to be received warmly by many people. It has been said that political discourse is unwelcome dinner conversation. This is all the more true about theology, for it deals with matters immeasurably more significant. Most people prefer to avoid talk of ultimate reality, precisely because such talk disrupts the comfortable preconceptions that allow us to sit at ease with the world and with ourselves. Nonetheless, the uneasiness cannot be avoided, nor should it be. If we are

---

23. Hans Boersma, *Heavenly Participation: The Weaving of a Sacramental Tapestry* (Grand Rapids: Eerdmans, 2011), 174.
24. Webster, *Confessing God*, 11 (emphasis added).

going to be converted to the truth, that conversion will sometimes be awkward, painful, inconvenient, and even unwelcome; but it will always be entirely worthwhile. God is *always* worth knowing.

There is a prayer in the Anglican tradition that wonderfully speaks to the purposes of this book. It is a prayer that occurs, fittingly, at the outset of the church's worship: "Almighty God, to you all hearts are open, all desires known, and from you no secrets are hid: Cleanse the thoughts of our hearts by the inspiration of your Holy Spirit, that we may perfectly love you, and worthily magnify your holy Name; through Christ our Lord. Amen."[25] Theology, after all, is a form of worship. So unless God cleanses our thoughts, by the power of the Spirit, in accordance with the revelation of the Lord Jesus, this work of theology, like any other, will have been in vain. Trusting in the grace of the Lord Jesus, we have designed this book as a call to Christian theological formation, as a way of faithfully indicating how theology shapes our understanding of reality because it expresses the truth.

To that end, the chapters in this book are ordered to reflect the primary substance, contexts, and character of theological study. They are meant to help orient the student of theology to the basic necessities and commitments of theology. Chapters 1 and 2 deal with the *substance* of theology, which is none other than the revelation of the incarnate Word of God in the person of our Lord Jesus Christ. Jesus determines reality because he is the full disclosure of the Creator and the full disclosure of all he created. Reality begins and ends with him. That reality, made known as we share the mind of Christ himself, ushers us into the truth and life of his Father through the Holy Spirit, so that our hearts and minds are conformed to God the Holy Trinity. Theology, we intend to show, is a sharing in the mind of Christ and thus has a distinctively trinitarian shape.

Chapters 3 and 4 deal with the *contexts* of theology, which are designated by the church and her ordered worship. The church is the

---

25. *The Book of Common Prayer* (New York: Oxford University Press, 1979), 355.

Christ-ordained location where Jesus promises to be truly present to sanctify his people through the ministries of Scripture and sacrament, conforming our hearts, minds, and bodies to the truth. In the preaching of the Word, through the waters of baptism, and by the partaking of the Lord's Supper, the body of Christ is given the gift of being conformed to the image of Christ. And it is in the worship and liturgy of the church that this astounding reality is brought to expression in our lives. Worshipful liturgy is the way that the church lives out her deepest commitments to reality, giving theological expression to the God-given rhythms of our daily lives. Theology, we aim to show, has both an ecclesial context and a liturgical cadence.

Chapters 5 and 6 deal with the *character* of Christian theology, demonstrating that Christian theology has both an inescapably paradoxical and mysterious quality and an inescapably eschatological tension. Theology entails paradox and mystery because it is always attentive to the fact that in the eternal Word made flesh the wisdom of God collides with the foolishness of men, disrupting preconceived notions of reality and exposing a chasm between our knowing and his. This is the chasm in which the mysterious and thus paradoxical nature of Christian confession is born—and where it truly thrives. Theology also possesses an eschatological character, because the renewal of our minds in Christ situates our confession of reality squarely in the eschatological tension of eternity-in-time, of the already and not-yet, of being in and for the world yet not of the world. The eschatological tension of Christian theology lends urgency and eternal significance to present action as the church lives between the two advents of our incarnate Lord.

Christians are called to the renewal and transformation of our minds in Christ Jesus in such a way that we are shaped to understand reality as it is determined by God. We believe that theology has a necessary part to play in that glorious reconfiguration. The study of theology is a gift God has given to his people through which we are granted the opportunity to reflect on, articulate, and contend for the faith "that was once for all delivered to the saints" (Jude 3).

This faith is the faith of the one, holy, catholic, apostolic church. The church is the grateful recipient of the gospel of our Lord Jesus as it is declared in, and always subject to, the Holy Scriptures. That is why all truly Christian theology, as we seek to express it in this book, must be distinctly *catholic* (in sympathetic acknowledgment of the historic witness of the church) and entirely *evangelical* (consistently attentive to the reforming fire of God's living and active Word). The Protestant theological commitments on display in this book, therefore, are Protestant precisely because they are at once both catholic and evangelical. Christian theology, whatever prior denominational commitments may obtain, is dependent on a reality that is a gift from God. Therefore, we are happy to press forward into our theological formation by affirming that "in the sphere of reality whose resplendent centre is Jesus Christ himself, God the Father has willed a knowledge of the Son of God which God the Holy Spirit has effected."[26] May the triune God of the gospel give in his infinite goodness what he has willed in his infinite wisdom!

---

26. Webster, *Confessing God*, 137.

Jesus Christ

The Lord and *Logos* of Christian Theology

Dorothy Sayers said it superbly: "The Christian faith is the most exciting drama that ever staggered the imagination of man—and the dogma *is* the drama. . . . The plot pivots upon a single character, and the whole action is the answer to a single central problem: *What think ye of Christ?*"[1] This is precisely the point Jesus sought to punctuate when asking his first disciples, "Who do people say that the Son of Man is?" Then, as now, public opinion varied wildly—from prophet to pariah, sage to simpleton, ally to enemy, and more besides. So Jesus pressed further, "But who do *you* say that I am?" With awed astonishment, Peter declared, "You are the Christ, the Son of the living God." An ordinary fisherman utters the definitive answer to the most crucial question ever posed, announcing nothing less than the meaning of reality, the fundamental fact of heaven and earth. On this confession Jesus builds his beloved church, against which nothing—not even the wiles of hell itself—shall prevail (Matt. 16:13–18; cf. Mark 8:27–29; Luke 9:18–20).

1. Dorothy L. Sayers, "The Greatest Drama Ever Staged," in *Creed or Chaos? Why Christians Must Choose Either Dogma or Disaster*, new and rev. ed. (Manchester, NH: Sophia Institute, 1999), 5 (emphasis original).

This scene is all the more striking because Jesus prompts Peter's confession at Caesarea Philippi, amid three prominent pagan shrines. One shrine was dedicated to Gad, the Canaanite god of good fortune; another was to Pan, the lustful Greek god of sex; and yet another was to the Roman Empire—the power of the state to solve all human problems. We would do well to recall that "what has been is what will be, and what has been done is what will be done, and there is nothing new under the sun" (Eccles. 1:9). For our present age routinely deifies self, sex, and the state—three of the most viscerally seductive and perennially pervasive substitutes for the triune God of the gospel—even if the shrines to this unholy trinity look different from before. All the while, Jesus continues to call his church. So in first and twenty-first centuries alike, his all-important, all-encompassing query—Who do *you* say that I am?—must be answered by each of us directly and personally amid the palpable presence of other gods, alien gospels, competing kingdoms, and conflicting claims to lordship.[2]

The call to Christian formation is the call of Christ to be formed in Christ. And this call necessarily entails *theological* formation, an invitation from the author and perfecter of our faith into a drama lovelier and livelier than any other (Heb. 12:1–2). Responding faithfully to this call is an act of humility that ennobles us, an act of devotion that costs us immensely yet enriches us immeasurably. And make no mistake: theological formation is the only antidote against being conformed to and deformed by the world, the only alternative to being catechized and liturgized by the spirit of the age and its dominant ways of thinking, speaking, and acting. For the rightful goal of theological formation is the renewal of our mind and transformation of our whole person into the image of our incarnate God and Savior (Rom. 12:1–2; 2 Cor. 3:18). So with awed astonishment of our own, let us ponder anew what it means that the Son of Man

2. Andrew Purves and Charles Partee, *Encountering God: Christian Faith in Turbulent Times* (Louisville: Westminster John Knox, 2000), 34–36; Anthony Esolen, *Out of the Ashes: Rebuilding American Culture* (Washington, DC: Regnery, 2017), 23.

is God the Son. Let us grasp with joyful confidence that Jesus Christ is the Lord and *Logos* of Christian theology.

Fully God, Fully Human

To confess that Jesus is the Son of the living God is to begin at the beginning. "In the beginning was the Word, and the Word was with God, and the Word was God" (John 1:1). Before all creaturely existence, before the creation of time itself, there was the eternal, uncreated life and light who is God the Holy Trinity; and there was the Word, the Second Person of the Trinity, ever with God as God. Note that John's Gospel begins by calling Jesus Christ both God and Word—in the original Greek, *Theos* and *Logos*. It is often said, and rightly so, that *theology* means a word about God. Yet John makes haste to indicate something much grander and more explicit: Jesus Christ is *himself* the substance and sum of our theology, in that this Word by God, from God, and about God *is* God the Word given for us, our blessed *Theos-Logos*. Further, *Logos* means speech, reason, and logic. So from the beginning, before time existed, the *Logos*, or Word, was the speech, the reason, and the logic of God—not an impersonal utterance or idea from God but the eternally begotten, eternally beloved Son of the Father. Eternity, then, is not an infinite and self-existent expanse of time. How horribly sterile and chilling that would be! Rather, eternity is the glorious life without beginning or end that God the Father and God the Son enjoy in the communion of God the Spirit—the very life that Jesus Christ has come to share with us (John 3:16; 17:3).

The church councils of Nicaea (325) and Constantinople (381) teach Scripture admirably, the latter heralding the Word as "the only-begotten Son of God, begotten from the Father before all time, Light from Light, true God from true God, begotten not created, of the same essence [reality] as the Father."[3] The procreation of human

---

3. "The Constantinopolitan Creed (381)," in *CC*, 33.

persons is bodily, occurs in time, and results in the separateness of begetter and begotten. But the Father begetting the Son is nonbodily and eternal, an internal event within God's life whereby the Father and Son are ever one in deity yet ever distinct in their uniqueness as Father and Son. Together with the Father and Spirit, the Son participates equally and eternally—truly, fully, and unreservedly—in God's triune life. The Son is thus inseparable from the Father and Spirit in both nature and action. For our triune God exists and acts triunely, in unity of divine nature with distinction of unique persons, and in unity of divine action with distinction of each person's unique ministry.[4]

Ever with God as God, the Word is God's self-expression.[5] As such, God's inner-triune life and light turned outward in self-giving love when the Word spoke all creation into existence, when the Son sang forth the cosmos. "In the beginning, God created the heavens and the earth" (Gen. 1:1). The first verse of John's Gospel echoes the first verse of Genesis to help us grasp that, in the beginning, "all things were made through him [the Word], and without him was not any thing made that was made. In him was life, and the life was the light of men" (John 1:3–4). Or as we read in Colossians, "For by him [Jesus Christ] all things were created, in heaven and on earth, visible and invisible . . . —all things were created through him and for him. And he is before all things, and in him all things hold together. . . . He is the beginning, . . . that in everything he might be preeminent" (Col. 1:16–18). The entire cosmos is from the Father through and for the Son, who is the agent and heir of all things. We inhabit an ordered universe, not a jumbled multiverse, because all created existence is grounded in Jesus Christ, who is the eternal and uncreated *Logos*, the very logic of creation (1 Cor. 8:6; Heb. 1:2; 11:3).[6]

The Word who spoke all things into existence was present to creation from its beginning, and remained so even after the world fell

---

4. Athanasius, *Against the Arians* 1.14–16, in *NPNF*², 4:314–16.

5. Michael Reeves, *Rejoicing in Christ* (Downers Grove, IL: IVP Academic, 2015), 13.

6. Athanasius, *Against the Heathen* 40–41, in *NPNF*², 4:25–26.

into sin. Because he refused to relinquish the object of God's holy love to dissolution and death, the same Word who enacted the creation of the cosmos also enacts its re-creation, fulfilling God's purpose for creation in redemption.[7] Note the Word's intimate involvement in the story of Israel, meeting Abraham's offspring at the Red Sea and Mount Sinai, abiding with them amid sojourn and settlement, and addressing them on the lips of priests and prophets (1 Cor. 10:1–4; 1 Pet. 1:10–11). Through tabernacle and temple, law and liturgy, the Word dwelt in their midst, his visage slowly yet surely emerging. Then at last, from the womb of Israel, the Word came forth to reveal the face of God in the face of Jesus, the Word made flesh. Indeed, Jesus Christ embodies the innermost reality of God, as he is that selfsame Word of God who has ever resided in the Father's bosom, who has ever resounded in the heart and depths of God's being (Exod. 33:18–20; John 1:14–18).[8]

Begotten of God his Father before time and begotten of Mary his mother in time, Jesus is both God the Son and Son of Man, dual citizen of heaven and earth. In other words, the eternal and uncreated Word is none other than Jesus the Christ—that son of Abraham who fulfills the messianic calling of Israel, and that son of Adam who alone is Savior of the world (Matt. 1:1–17; Mark 1:1; Luke 1:35; 3:23–38). The church council of Chalcedon (451) faithfully articulates the mystery of the Word made flesh, confessing that Jesus Christ is

> perfect both in deity and also in human-ness. . . . He is of the same reality as God as far as his deity is concerned and of the same reality as we are ourselves as far as his human-ness is concerned; thus like us in all respects, sin only excepted. Before time began he was begotten of the Father, in respect of his deity, and now in these last days, for us and on behalf of our salvation, this selfsame one was born of Mary the virgin, who is God-bearer in respect of his human-ness. . . . We

---

7. Colin Gunton, "And in One Lord, Jesus Christ . . . Begotten, Not Made," in *Nicene Christianity: The Future for a New Ecumenism*, ed. Christopher R. Seitz (Grand Rapids: Brazos, 2001), 42–45.

8. Reeves, *Rejoicing in Christ*, 13–14.

apprehend this one and only Christ—Son, Lord, only-begotten—in
two natures; without confusing the two natures, without transmuting
one nature into the other, without dividing them into two separate
categories, without contrasting them according to area or function.
The distinctiveness of each nature is not nullified by the union. Instead,
the properties of each nature are conserved and both natures concur
in one person. . . . They are not divided . . . but are together the one
and only and only-begotten Logos of God, the Lord Jesus Christ.[9]

Here the church unabashedly asserts what one twentieth-century
luminary lauds as the great scandal of metaphysics: Jesus Christ partakes simultaneously and unreservedly in the being and life of both
deity and humanity. Remaining God in the heart of the unchanged
Trinity, the eternal Word became what he created without ceasing to
be who he has ever been, such that in Jesus, God's deity includes our
humanity.[10] From the moment of his conception in the womb of Mary,
God the Son has deigned to live his divine life evermore in our human
nature. The Word took the whole of our human constitution into
his divine self to be our Immanuel, God with us as one of us (Matt.
1:23). He entered the deepest ground of our being and engaged our
situation east of Eden even unto death, that he might heal us at the
root of our corruption and alienation by mediating the life of God
to us in and as man.[11] The grand reality that God the Son is the Son
of Man does not undermine his deity or his humanity. It does not
obliterate the distinction between his divine and human natures, nor
does it suggest a divisible, disintegrated patchwork of natures that
render him only intermittently, alternately divine and human. Rather,
deity and humanity are inextricably united and wholly preserved

9. "The Definition of Chalcedon (451)," in CC, 35–36.
10. Vladimir Lossky, Orthodox Theology: An Introduction, trans. Ian Kesarcodi-
Watson and Ihita Kesarcodi-Watson (Crestwood, NY: St. Vladimir's Seminary Press,
1978), 91.
11. Our Lord transforms what he touches, saving us as whole persons by assuming
our human nature not in part but in whole. He assumes to heal and heals by assuming.
See Gregory of Nazianzus, "To Cledonius the Priest against Apollinarius," Letters
on the Apollinarian Controversy, no. 101, in NPNF², 7:440.

in the person of Jesus the God-man, who concurrently does divine things humanly and human things divinely, exuding the re-creative freedom of God's almighty love in human acts of limitless significance and consequence.[12]

Do not miss that precisely, explicitly as the fully *human* Son of Man is the eternal Word the image of God, the exact imprint of God's nature, and the One in whom the whole fullness of deity dwells bodily (2 Cor. 4:4; Col. 1:15, 19; 2:9; Heb. 1:3). For the enfleshment of the *Logos* neither contradicts nor obscures who God is, as if God were known more fully and clearly prior to or apart from the appearing of Immanuel. When God the Son assumed our humanity, it was by no means an instance of divine retreat or regressive revelation. Far from it! This astonishing act of divine invasion, of progressive revelation, is God's ultimate unveiling, in that Jesus is the very radiance of God's glory (Heb. 1:3). And this apex of divine condescension displays not God's self-abdication but his omnipotent self-possession. For God's accommodation to our humanness in the fully human Jesus does not diminish his divine majesty in the least. Quite the opposite, this is God's freely chosen way of exalting his divine majesty, of exhibiting that God's self-emptying and self-fulfillment are not antithetical but identical (Phil. 2:5–11). To confess the union of God and humanity in the God-man is thus to confess that Jesus is at once truly and fully God as true and full human, that what he does and says as a human, he does and says as God.[13] Jesus Christ, then, is even more than the substance and sum of our theology. He is the ultimate theologian, the only human who speaks about God, on behalf of God, *as God*. And for this reason the Father adjures, "This is my Son, my Chosen One; listen to him!" (Luke 9:35).

---

12. David S. Yeago, "Crucified Also for Us under Pontius Pilate: Six Propositions on the Preaching of the Cross," in Seitz, *Nicene Christianity*, 92.

13. John Webster, "Incarnation," in *The Blackwell Companion to Modern Theology*, ed. Gareth Jones (Oxford: Blackwell, 2004), 218; John C. Clark and Marcus Peter Johnson, *The Incarnation of God: The Mystery of the Gospel as the Foundation of Evangelical Theology* (Wheaton: Crossway, 2015), 80–82.

The Key That Unlocks the Whole of Reality

Jesus Christ is the imagination-staggering singularity at the center of all that is. So what does this mean for our understanding of God, humanity, and the world, for our understanding of theology? It means that if we want to say true things about the way things truly are, we must join John Williamson Nevin in praising the incarnate Word as the key that unlocks the sense of all God's revelations and works.[14] For God the Son entered the world as the Son of Man so that God, humanity, and the world may have full and final, concrete and definitive, revelation in him. Jesus unites in himself deity and humanity, Creator and creation, eternity and time, heaven and earth, bringing to light a reality that is both integral and intelligible, not dichotomous and disjointed. And Jesus reveals not many realities with multiple ways of access to them but one reality discerned relative to himself. Therefore, any outlook that fails to see and savor all things in Christ and Christ in all things is not a truly Christian outlook on reality but an abstraction from reality—a fictitious, virtual reality. To contemplate the world *in Christ* is to gain true knowledge of both God and the world. To contemplate the world *apart from Christ* is to forfeit true knowledge of both God and the world. Dietrich Bonhoeffer thus asserted:

> The place where the questions about the reality of God and about the reality of the world are answered at the same time is characterized solely by the name: Jesus Christ. God and the world are enclosed in this name. . . . We cannot speak rightly of either God or the world without speaking of Jesus Christ. All concepts of reality that ignore Jesus Christ are abstractions. . . . There are not two realities, but *only one reality*, and that is God's reality revealed in Christ in the reality of the world. . . . The reality of Christ embraces the reality of the world in itself. The world has no reality of its own independent of

14. John Williamson Nevin, *The Mystical Presence: A Vindication of the Reformed or Calvinistic Doctrine of the Holy Eucharist* (Philadelphia: J. B. Lippencott, 1846), 199.

God's revelation in Christ. It is a denial of God's revelation in Jesus Christ to wish to be "Christian" without being "worldly," or wish to be worldly without seeing and recognizing the world in Christ. Hence there are not two realms, but only *the one realm of the Christ-reality*, in which the reality of God and the reality of the world are united.[15]

Jesus placed the triune name of Father, Son, and Spirit forever on the church's heart and lips (Matt. 28:18–20). He is that Word who is ever in the Father, just as the Father is ever in him. So the Father sending the Son to the world is not the Father sending the Son away from himself but the Father drawing near to us through the Son. Jesus came into the world to make the Father known, to reveal that knowledge of the Father through the Son and knowledge of the Son from the Father are one—that to behold the Son *is* to behold the Father (John 10:30; 12:44–45; 14:8–11). Irenaeus said it well: "The Father is the invisible of the Son, but the Son the visible of the Father."[16] And the same is true of the Spirit. Jesus acts in the power of the Spirit, gives the Spirit in his name, and details the ministry of the Spirit in relation to himself, such that he is no less the visible of the Spirit than he is the visible of the Father. Indeed, Jesus reveals that knowledge of the Spirit through the Son and knowledge of the Son by the Spirit are one—that to behold the Son *is* to behold the Spirit (John 14:26; 15:26; 16:13–15). Vladimir Lossky was right: "All that we know of the Trinity we know through the Incarnation."[17]

Who God has ever been in his inner-triune life he now is and evermore shall be to us in the incarnate Son. True knowledge of Jesus is true knowledge of the Father and Spirit, such that knowing Jesus is what it means to know God, not just the first step toward or an additional step beyond knowing God. To see, hear, and receive Immanuel

---

15. Dietrich Bonhoeffer, *Ethics*, ed. Clifford J. Green, trans. Reinhard Krauss et al., vol. 6 of *Dietrich Bonhoeffer Works*, ed. Wayne Whitson Floyd Jr. and Victoria J. Barnett (Minneapolis: Fortress, 2005), 54, 58 (emphasis original).

16. Irenaeus, *Against Heresies* 4.6.6, in *ANF*, 1:469.

17. Lossky, *Orthodox Theology*, 90.

is to see, hear, and receive not a part of God but the fullness of God. This means there is absolutely no search to undertake for God, and no appeal to make to God, over the head or behind the back of Jesus, the perfect expression of who God is in himself. Michael Ramsey put it beautifully: "God is Christlike, and in him is no un-Christlikeness at all."[18] Because the Son is of the same divine reality as the Father and Spirit, the Father sending the Son in the power of the Spirit is nothing less, different, or other than the self-giving of God as God has always been and will forever be.[19]

Bonhoeffer is spot-on: the reality of God is characterized by Jesus Christ. And the same is true of humanity. In other words, given that Jesus is perfect in both deity and humanity, he is the definitive expression of both deity and humanity, revealing both *God* to us and *us* to us, both God's self and our self. For this reason Blaise Pascal sagely stated, "Not only do we only know God through Jesus Christ, but we only know ourselves through Jesus Christ."[20] The first thing Scripture says about humans is that we are unique among all creatures because we alone are the image of God. The true measure of a worm is a worm; the true measure of a fish is a fish; the true measure of a bird is a bird; and the true measure of a beast is a beast. *But the true measure of a human is God* (Gen. 1:20–27). Yet what does it mean that even the first humans were created in the image of God when—prior to the incarnation—there was categorically, qualitatively *nothing* human about God?

The apostle Paul uses two designations to highlight that *the true measure of a human is God as human, the human God*: image of the invisible God, and firstborn of all creation (Col. 1:15). Jesus is

18. Michael Ramsey, *God, Christ and the World: A Study in Contemporary Theology* (London: SCM, 1969), 98.

19. Thomas F. Torrance, *The Trinitarian Faith: The Evangelical Theology of the Ancient Catholic Church* (London: T&T Clark, 1991), 132–45; Colin Gunton, *Act and Being: Towards a Theology of the Divine Attributes* (Grand Rapids: Eerdmans, 2003), 93–98.

20. Blaise Pascal, *Pensées*, trans. A. J. Krailsheimer (New York: Penguin, 1995), no. 417, p. 141.

the image of the invisible God, the fullness of God in whom there is *everything* human. He is the standard of our image bearing, the proper datum point and controlling principle for understanding authentic human existence. For Jesus is not simply an inheritor of a humanity that existed before the incarnation but the ground and interpretive paradigm for a humanity that is not self-referential or self-explanatory. The definitive image of God, Jesus is the firstborn of all creation, which refers not to birth order but to supremacy of status. Before and above all things, as the agent and heir of all creation, he fashioned even the first humans in accordance with and anticipation of the divine image he would become in the fullness of time as the God-man. As the redeemer of humanity, Jesus is indeed the second Adam (Rom. 5:12–21; 1 Cor. 15:21–22, 45); but as a template for humanity, the first Adam is the second image-firstborn.[21] In other words, Jesus is the *antitype* of Adam and the *archetype* of humanity—the model or pattern for all other humans. Irenaeus echoes Paul when declaring, "For in times long past, it was *said* that man was created after the image of God, but it was not [actually] *shown*; for the Word was as yet invisible, after whose image man was created. . . . When, however, the Word of God became flesh, He . . . showed forth the image truly, since He became Himself what was His image."[22]

Jesus Christ is the true measure of a human; he alone reveals the truth about humanity. To miss Jesus is thus to mask the ground and goal of human existence, since we were fashioned after him for conformity to him. But to receive Jesus is to have him scatter the darkness of our hearts with the light of his life-giving presence, so that we learn *who* we are by learning *whose* we are (John 1:4–5; 3:19–21; 8:12; 2 Cor. 4:6). This happens not by psychological introspection or therapeutic technique but by discovering our true self in union with Jesus, by discerning our authentically human face in the face of Christ. For the cramped circumference of a false self is graciously

---

21. Scot McKnight, *The Letter to the Colossians*, New International Commentary on the New Testament (Grand Rapids: Eerdmans, 2018), 145–49.
22. Irenaeus, *Against Heresies* 5.16.2, in *ANF*, 1:544 (emphasis original).

opened up to include Christ's self, so that self-understanding is reconstituted as our identity is forged in and drawn from Christ (Gal. 2:20). Jesus reveals *us* to us by rectifying the sin-riddled relationship we have with ourselves, marked by our hearts being curved in on themselves in a labyrinth of our own contriving. As such, true knowledge of self is brought about not by self-analysis but by God's self-disclosure in Christ.[23]

Recall Bonhoeffer's avowal that we can speak rightly of the world only by speaking rightly of Christ, that the whole of creation has no reality of its own—no independent existence or true intelligibility—apart from the one *Christ-reality*. What could possibly be more thrilling? All creation exists because of Christ and for Christ. Reality in Christ thus entails redemption, yet it extends beyond redemption to the reason creation exists in the first place—to the reason that God created all things rather than nothing at all (Col. 1:16; cf. John 1:3; 1 Cor. 8:6; Heb. 1:1–2).[24] So here we must grasp that the incarnation is not a divine afterthought, no mere emergency measure to counteract sin and evil. It is not the case that God created all things because of Christ and for Christ yet with the intent that Christ would never be born—with the intent that the *eternal* Word would never become the *incarnate* Word. For the incarnate Word reveals the eternal Trinity, that God's name has ever been Father, Son, and Spirit. The incarnate Word reveals the true measure of humanity, that the dignity and nobility of our divine image bearing has always meant being patterned after the God-man. And the incarnate Word reveals the true meaning of the world, that from the dawn of creation he has been its origin and aim. Indeed, the world was made so Christ could be born, so Jesus could be the Alpha and Omega, the selfsame Word who called

23. Julie Canlis, *Calvin's Ladder: A Spiritual Theology of Ascent and Ascension* (Grand Rapids: Eerdmans, 2010), 114–15; Canlis, "John Calvin: Knowing the Self in God's Presence," in *Sources of the Christian Self: A Cultural History of Christian Identity*, ed. James M. Houston and Jens Zimmermann (Grand Rapids: Eerdmans, 2018), 410.

24. McKnight, *Letter to the Colossians*, 150.

forth and consummates the cosmos (John 1:1; Rev. 1:8; 19:13; 21:6; 22:13).[25] It was established before the foundation of the world that Christ would be the Lamb slain for our salvation. But this does not mean that the reason for the incarnation is simply sin and evil. Rather, it means that God is loath to let sin and evil thwart his eternal plan to create the world so Christ could be one with us as one of us, even if our breaking the world and breaking ourselves requires the breaking of Christ's body (Acts 2:22–24; 1 Pet. 1:18–20; Rev. 13:8).

God's transcendent truth, goodness, and beauty open up in the world through Christ. All things hold together in him who is preeminent in everything, who is healing this fallen world as the firstfruits of fully uniting heaven and earth in himself (Eph. 1:10; Col. 1:17–20). Jesus brings heaven to bear on earth to penetrate and permeate earth with heaven; and thus he inaugurates for his church on earth a participatory connection—a holy communion—with heaven that even now is profoundly real (Eph. 1:3; 2:6; Phil. 3:20; Col. 3:1). Knowing Christ as the ground and goal of creation frees us to duly value and truly enjoy earthly realities, because we learn that earthly realities are not ends in themselves but means whose end is the one *Christ-reality*. In other words, earthly realities are God-given gifts whose God-intended aim is "that knowledge which is communion, and . . . that communion which fulfills itself as true knowledge: knowledge of God and therefore knowledge of the world."[26] This knowledge safeguards us from the tandem temptations to either devalue earthly realities as trivial or idolize them as ultimate. Further, this knowledge exposes modern secularism as a peculiar and pernicious sort of flat-earth society that exhibits a pathological impulse to rip earth from heaven and then flatten the vertical dimension of earth—to reduce a God-ordered, God-enchanted creation to mere nature and then

25. David Fergusson, "Creation," in *The Oxford Handbook of Systematic Theology*, ed. John Webster, Kathryn Tanner, and Iain Torrance (New York: Oxford University Press, 2007), 76–77.

26. Alexander Schmemann, *For the Life of the World: Sacraments and Orthodoxy*, 2nd ed. (Crestwood, NY: St. Vladimir's Seminary Press, 2002), 120.

perceive nature as a malleable, self-enclosed plaything to objectify, deconstruct, and redefine at whim.[27]

The flat-earth society that is modern secularism tells a tragic tale of an abstract concept of reality that attempts to impose its own agenda on the world, because it refuses to recognize the world in Christ. Here, then, is a case in point for the fact that precisely as Jesus is the light who reveals the true meaning of the world, he exposes the true character of what Scripture often calls the *powers* (Rom. 8:38–39; 1 Cor. 15:24; Eph. 1:21; 2:1–2; 6:12; Col. 1:16; 2:15). These are the forces of darkness at work in this fallen world—manifestations of cosmic rebellion against Christ embedded in the cultural, ideological, sociopolitical structures of our earthly existence. Together they constitute the spirit of the age—the world, the flesh, and the devil—that we must always and everywhere renounce and resist (1 Pet. 5:8–9; 1 John 2:15–17). On life as a university student in Hitler-led Germany prior to the Second World War, Hendrik Berkhof recalls, "No one could withhold himself, without utmost effort, from the grasp these Powers had on men's inner and outer life. . . . They acted as if they were ultimate values, calling for loyalty as if they were the gods of the cosmos."[28] And lest we indulge that self-righteous pleasure of puzzling over the evil that all-too-conveniently assails other times, other places, and other people, Berkhof adds: "Nor should it be difficult for us to perceive today in every realm of life these Powers which unify men, yet separate them from God. The state, politics, class, social struggle, national interest, public opinion, accepted morality, the ideas of decency, humanity, democracy—these give unity and direction to . . . [many] lives. Yet precisely by giving unity and direction they separate these many lives from the true God; they let us believe that we have found the meaning of existence, whereas they really estrange us from true meaning."[29]

27. Hans Boersma, "Reconnecting the Threads: Theology as Sacramental Tapestry," *Crux* 47, no. 3 (Fall 2011): 32–37.

28. Hendrik Berkhof, *Christ and the Powers*, trans. John H. Yoder (Kitchener, ON: Herald, 1977), 32.

29. Berkhof, *Christ and the Powers*, 32–33.

The Heart of the Matter

In Jesus Christ the reality of God entered the reality of the world in the reality of our humanity. This is a game changer beyond compare! For it means that true knowledge of God, humanity, and the world comes from the God who bursts the wineskins of the world in the fully human Jesus. It means that only communion with the God-man amid the world fulfills itself in true knowledge of God, humanity, and the world, in true knowledge of the one *Christ-reality*. In other words, it means that reality must be understood theologically, because reality is inherently theological. And this happens when Jesus opens reality to us as only he can—for he is not only the substance and sum of theology; he is the ultimate theologian. So here we come to the heart of the matter: Jesus Christ is the Lord and *Logos* of all things, and thus he alone is the Lord and *Logos* of Christian theology.

"Jesus is Lord!" is the church's primary confession, and it involves a twofold claim (Rom. 10:9; 1 Cor. 12:3; 2 Cor. 4:5; Phil. 2:11). First, this joyful and exuberant claim specifies Jesus's relationship to the God of Israel and the Old Testament. For the apostles seized on the title *kyrios*—Lord—used to translate God's sacred name from the Hebrew Scriptures into Greek, and they applied it to Jesus throughout the New Testament (e.g., Rom. 1:7; 5:1; 1 Cor. 1:10; 8:6; Eph. 1:2–3; 4:4–6; Phil. 3:8; Col. 2:6; Heb. 13:20; James 2:1; 1 Pet. 1:3; 3:15; Rev. 1:8). As such, the apostolic confession that Jesus is Lord echoes Jesus in equating him with the God revealed to the Hebrew patriarchs as Yahweh, the great I Am (Exod. 3:14; John 8:58). To say that Jesus is Lord is thus to say that Jesus is *God*. Second, this humble and repentant claim specifies singular and exclusive devotion to One whose lordship is unique, unqualified, and universal.[30] The apostles do not add a caveat to the claim that Jesus is Lord, as if he were only a tribal, provincial deity of certain people or portions of existence.

---

30. Alister E. McGrath, *Understanding Doctrine: What It Is—and Why It Matters* (Grand Rapids: Zondervan, 1990), 123; Larry W. Hurtado, *Lord Jesus Christ: Devotion to Jesus in Earliest Christianity* (Grand Rapids: Eerdmans, 2003), 108–18.

So let us be clear: to confess that Jesus is Lord is to heartily affirm Jesus's teaching that all authority in heaven and on earth is his alone (Matt. 28:18). It is to happily reject all other so-called lords in the liberating acknowledgment that his lordship is every bit as extensive as his creation and renewal of all things. For our Lord Jesus "is the incomparably comprehensive context of all creaturely being, knowing and acting, because in and as him God is with humankind in free, creative, and saving love."[31]

Because our Lord is the divine Word with us as the all-encompassing context of created existence, he is the *Logos*—indeed, the very logic—of reality. Therefore, authentically Christian theology is unabashedly *Christ-ian* theology, repudiating every pressure to lay any foundation in place or alongside of that which is laid: the mighty bulwark who is Jesus Christ (1 Cor. 3:11). We have a splendid example of just this sort of repudiation in the Barmen Declaration, prompted by the rise of the Third Reich in prewar Germany. With sublime faith and fortitude, it proclaims:

> Jesus Christ, as he is testified to us in the Holy Scripture, is the one Word of God, whom we are to hear, whom we are to trust and obey in life and in death. We repudiate the false teaching that the church can and must recognize yet other happenings and powers, images and truths as divine revelation alongside this one Word of God. . . . Just as Jesus Christ is the pledge of the forgiveness of all our sins, just so— and with the same earnestness—is he also God's mighty claim on our whole life; in him we encounter a joyous liberation from the godless claims of this world to free and thankful service to his creatures. We repudiate the false teaching that there are areas of our life in which we belong not to Jesus Christ but another lord. . . . With her faith as well as her obedience, with her message as well as her ordinances, [the Christian church] has to witness in the midst of the world of sin as the church of forgiven sinners that she is his alone, that she lives and wishes to live only by his comfort and his counsel in expectation of

31. Webster, "Incarnation," 204.

his appearance. We repudiate the false teaching that the church can turn over the form of her message and ordinances at will or according to some dominant ideological and political convictions.[32]

The church's only head is Jesus Christ. She is sourced in this one Word of God, abides in this Word, and will not heed the cacophonous din of strange voices swirling around her. This one Word of God—the only Lord and *Logos* of Christian theology—calls his church in every age and circumstance to stand and not fall, to be confident and not anxious, to confess and not be silent, to resist and not conform to anything or anyone but him. For Jesus is not one Word among other possibilities but the light of the world who alone dispels its lies, the life of the world who alone disempowers its death (John 10:1–15; 12:35–50; 15:1–25; 16:25–33).[33] Therefore, truly *Christ-ian* theology is never a word in advance of or apart from this one Word of God but is always a word in response to the Word, enabled solely by that Word. Truly *Christ-ian* theology is the church's devoted answer to a divine address, our rapt rejoinder to being sought and sustained by the Word who calls and claims us as his dearly beloved.

Theology whose Lord and *Logos* is Christ cannot be an exercise in which we step outside the presence of divine revelation, the practice of faith and worship, or participation in the life of the church to adopt some abstract and supposedly objective stance toward the one Word of God, as if this Word were merely another object at our disposal. For theology's warrant can never be found in human capacity, popular spirituality, perceived public relevance, or pathetic attempts to placate cultural values. Instead, theology's warrant is predicated only and ever on the triune God's presence in the church—revealed through the Son by the Spirit and testified to us in Scripture. Other enterprises are often called theology, but they are something quite

32. "The Barmen Declaration (1934)," in *CC*, 520–21.
33. Eberhard Busch, *The Barmen Theses Then and Now*, trans. Darrell Guder and Judith Guder (Grand Rapids: Eerdmans, 2010), 21–23.

other than *Christ-ian*.[34] These are little more than thinly veiled ways
of "not holding fast to the Head" (Col. 2:19)—ploys to resist and
evade Jesus Christ, to flee him under the guise of seeking him. Such
is the subtle allure and abiding temptation of every "theologian who
tries to encounter Christ and yet to avoid that encounter. . . . Christ is
still betrayed by the kiss. Wishing to be done with him means always
to fall down with the mockers and say, 'Greetings, Master!'"[35]

Christian theology does not seek knowledge of God apart from
God or on any ground but the one Word of God. For God alone reveals God, and Christ is God's self-expression. This one Word is the
God-given surety from which theology must begin, not simply the
plausible end at which theology attempts to arrive. For theology's end
depends on its beginning. Jesus is the perfecter of our faith precisely
because he is the author of our faith (Heb. 12:2); he is the Omega
precisely because he is the Alpha (Rev. 1:8; 21:6); and he is the one
Word who judges all things in the end precisely because he is the one
Word who created all things in the beginning (John 1:1–3; Rev. 19:13).
Our Lord is the *Logos* of God's self-disclosure and the logic of all
creation, so the conditions of theology must ever be set by him, *never
by the world or the church*. To be sure, theology adores Christ and
adorns his church only when the living Truth himself establishes the
character of this holy vocation—only when theology is a servant of
the one Word of God, not his self-appointed master.

Theology stands in suspicion and incredulity toward its Lord—
that perverse posture of self-lordship—when it prescribes methods of
its own choosing and grants them an independent and authoritarian
role in this God-given vocation.[36] It is folly in the fullest to presume
or pretend that there are responses to Christ's lordship besides the

34. John Webster, *Holiness* (Grand Rapids: Eerdmans, 2003), 12–15; Murray Rae,
"Prolegomena," in *Trinitarian Soundings in Systematic Theology*, ed. Paul Louis
Metzger (London: T&T Clark, 2006), 9–11.

35. Dietrich Bonhoeffer, *Christ the Center*, trans. Edwin H. Robertson (New York:
Harper & Row, 1978), 35.

36. Thomas F. Torrance, *The School of Faith: The Catechisms of the Reformed
Church* (New York: Harper, 1959), l.

bent knee or the brandished fist, some other sort of reply than "Let it be to me according to your word" or "Crucify, crucify him!" (Luke 1:38; 23:21). Unserious souls will protest and feign otherwise; they always have. But Bonhoeffer knew better: "There are only two ways possible of encountering Jesus: man must die or he must put Jesus to death."[37] Those who practice *Christ-ian* theology bear the blessed marks of the former, marks of being put to death and raised to new life by the holy and merciful Word for the praise of God and service to the church. For they have learned that, because Jesus is Lord, "he can only be thought of as Lord; if he is not thought of as Lord, and with the rational deference which is due to him as Lord, then he is not thought of at all."[38]

One God, One Mediator: The Way, Truth, and Life

The faith that was once and for all delivered to the saints attests that "there is one God, and there is one mediator between God and men, the man Christ Jesus" (1 Tim. 2:5). Now as then, however, the faithful confess one God and one mediator amid a context cluttered with counterfeit gods and mediators. Martin Luther's insight is ageless: "Anything on which your heart relies and depends, . . . that is really your God."[39] All people espouse some deity or another, which they trust and obey in some form or another. Moderns who deny the existence of all gods in the proper sense do nothing to discredit this claim. Quite the contrary, they demonstrate that human nature, like all nature, abhors vacuums—that human nature, in the words of John Calvin, is a "factory of idols."[40] For these denials only prompt appeals to alternative authorities, substitute and surrogate deities—whatever is deemed ultimate in its ability to open reality and give meaning to existence. In effect, then, even so-called godless ideologies,

---

37. Bonhoeffer, *Christ the Center*, 35.
38. Webster, "Incarnation," 206.
39. Martin Luther, "The Large Catechism (1529)," in *BC*, 386.
40. John Calvin, *Inst.* 1.11.8.

like those advanced in naturalistic approaches to the sciences or in social-constructionist approaches to philosophy, history, literature, race and gender studies, and other areas of the humanities, are necessarily religious and theological in nature. Humans are hardwired for worship, so worship we will. The question is not *whether* we will worship; it is who or what we will worship, and to what end.[41]

Yet most people are *not* atheists. And while some people form convictions with immense industry, many do not. The influences that most deeply and directly shape their convictions do not come first and foremost from libraries, learned tomes, or lecterns. Instead, these influences are embedded in and emerge from culture, and they are imbibed—casually and subtly—through the informal catechesis of cultural contact and the latent liturgies that lend structure and rhythm to life. Inhaled with the air, reaped from the soil of daily routines, the messaging of modernity is absorbed through media, at malls, in movie theaters, and over meals at school and work. What most powerfully affects the convictions of many people is more caught than taught, more lived than learned, in any formal sense. But regardless of how our convictions are formed, they constitute the basic commitments of our hearts. Scripture thus warns, "Keep your heart with all vigilance, for from it flow the springs of life" (Prov. 4:23). For good or ill, the commitments of our hearts tell us what to trust and fear, love and loath, value and revile, adore and abhor. They decide what we deem beautiful and ugly, good and evil—what we care a great deal about, and about what we care nothing at all. They direct our attempts to satisfy our deepest human desires. They diagnose our most pressing problems and their solutions—determining who or what we will worship and where we will seek salvation.[42]

41. Karl Barth, *Evangelical Theology: An Introduction*, trans. Grover Foley (Grand Rapids: Eerdmans, 1979), 3–4. For an impressive examination of the oft-veiled yet invariably theological nature of all human theorizing, see Roy A. Clouser, *The Myth of Religious Neutrality: An Essay on the Hidden Role of Religious Belief in Theories*, rev. ed. (Notre Dame, IN: University of Notre Dame Press, 2005), chaps. 7–9.

42. Steve Wilkens and Mark L. Sanford, *Hidden Worldviews: Eight Cultural Stories That Shape Our Lives* (Downers Grove, IL: IVP Academic, 2009), 11–26.

All the while, Jesus calls his church to a theological formation that must be proactively, persistently, even pugnaciously lived out amid pressure to be conformed to and deformed by the world, to be catechized and liturgized by the spirit of the age. So like the saints in every age, we must keep our hearts with all vigilance in a landscape littered with would-be gods and mediators. To name just a few: If the god is materialism, the mediator is money. If the god is inner-psychic serenity, the mediator is therapy. If the god is naturalism, the mediator is the denatured science of scientism. If the god is the diversion of feast and frolic, the mediator is the entertainment empire. If the god is self-definition, the mediator is self-preoccupation. If the god is limitless sexual expression, the mediator is endless sexual revolution. If the god is progressive statism, the mediator is political activism. If the god is the celestial brain of rationalism, the mediator is the cerebral hubris of intellectualism. If the god is some mute, distant designer of the cosmos, the mediator is creation. But if the God is the one and only true God—the living, speaking, triune God who reveals himself through himself—the one and only mediator is none other than Jesus Christ.

And Jesus Christ is not simply the one and only mediator *from* God *to* men, but the one and only mediator *between* God *and* men (1 Tim. 2:5). That is to say, his mediation is not simply one-directional but is bidirectional. The English Reformer Richard Hooker stated this art-fully, noting that there could be "no union of God with man without that mean between both which is both."[43] His point: there is union between God and humanity precisely because Jesus unites God with humanity by partaking wholly and at once in the being and life of both God and humanity as the God-man. Jesus brings God to humans and humans to God. For he is God with humanity on behalf of God, and humanity with God on behalf of humanity—the complete form of God's revealing, reconciling action to humanity, and the perfect

43. Richard Hooker, *Laws of Ecclesiastical Polity* 5.50.3 in *The Works of That Learned and Judicious Divine Mr. Richard Hooker* (Oxford: Clarendon, 1865), 2:220.

form of humanity's response to God. From the side of God, Jesus acts as light and life to humanity; and from the side of humanity, he acts in unswerving trust, obedience, and adoration to the Father in the power of the Spirit.[44] Our one and only mediator came in the name of the Father, conceived by and endowed with the Spirit, to live and act in our name, to flawlessly fulfill all divine righteousness as our fully human representative and substitute. He assumed the whole of our humanness so that, in solidarity with us as one of us, he might be for us who we could not be and do for us what we could not do. Jesus was born for us, baptized for us, bested temptation for us, lived for us, died for us, rose to unending life for us, opened heaven in his ascended body for us, and presently intercedes for us, so that all he renders to the Father in our place and stead is thereby rendered ours.

Hans Urs von Balthasar rightly exults: "Myth is unmasked by the Word of God."[45] We do not demythologize Jesus Christ; he demythologizes us, exposing the groundless lies that enthrall us, among them the vanity-laden fantasy of secular progress—the modern myth that humanity has at last come into its own on its own. Stunningly, however, Jesus does this demythologizing not by rejecting our humanity but by assuming our humanity and making it his own. He is thus the fount of all God's blessings, and the divine gifts he shares with us result from the humanity we share with him. Our mediator has come clothed in the gospel to humanly mediate the gifts that are his alone to give. And we receive those gifts only by receiving Jesus himself, only by participating in the risen life of our incarnate substitute. In the emphatic words of Calvin,

> How do we receive those benefits which the Father bestowed on his only-begotten Son—not for Christ's own private use, but that he might

44. Thomas F. Torrance, *Royal Priesthood: A Theology of Ordained Ministry*, 2nd ed. (London: T&T Clark, 1993), 1–13.

45. Hans Urs von Balthasar, introduction to *The Scandal of the Incarnation: Irenaeus "Against the Heresies,"* by Irenaeus, trans. John Saward (San Francisco: Ignatius, 1990), 6.

enrich poor and needy men? First, we must understand that as long as Christ remains outside of us, and we are separated from him, all that he has suffered and done for the salvation of the human race remains useless and of no value for us. Therefore, to share with us what he has received from the Father, he had to become ours and to dwell within us. For this reason, he is called "our Head" [Eph. 4:15], and "the first-born among many brethren" [Rom. 8:29]. We also, in turn, are said to be "engrafted into him" [Rom. 11:17], and to "put on Christ" [Gal. 3:27]; for, as I have said, all that he possesses is nothing to us until we grow into one body with him.[46]

Jesus ever lives and acts *for us*, but not to render him remote or absent *from us*. Quite the contrary, the Word became flesh so we may evermore dwell in him and he in us—so our every lack may find its remedy in the fullness of our fully human mediator. God the Son became the Son of Man "to impart to us what was his, and to become both Son of God and Son of man in common with us."[47] This union with Christ entails the whole of the believer's humanity, not least a participation in the very *mind* of Christ, a sharing in the eternal love-and-devotion-drenched knowing of the Father that by nature is the Son's alone. Jesus is utterly clear that "no one knows the Father except the Son and anyone to whom the Son chooses to reveal him" (Matt. 11:27; cf. Luke 10:22). No human except the incarnate Son enjoys unmediated knowledge of God, so our knowledge of God can have no ground or center but the Son. This knowledge cannot be directly drawn from the world, nor can it be developed from our innate human capacities. For it results only from an epistemic transformation of the believer's whole person—intellect, will, affect, and imagination—from the profound reorientation and renewal of one's mind in the mind of Christ.

Christian theology thus results from our participation in the life of the incarnate *Logos*, such that our thinking, speaking, and acting

46. Calvin, *Inst.* 3.1.1.
47. Calvin, *Inst.* 2.12.2.

reflect not an arbitrary logic alien to the *Logos* but that of the *Logos* himself. Of course, participation in Christ is not the same as being Christ. Our knowledge of God is not the deification of reason. Nor is it the abandonment of reason or an addition to reason. It is the *redemption* of our reason as Christ draws us by the Spirit into his communion with the Father, granting us real yet mediated knowledge of God in keeping with the infinite qualitative difference between God and the living members of his body.[48] In other words, participating in Christ means that we have been slain and made alive in our cruci- fied and risen Lord, that our minds are being sanctified and healed, conformed to and transformed by our ascended Lord's own human mind as we partake through him in the eternal life he shares with the Father and Spirit. Keith Johnson writes:

> How we know God by our participation in the life of God through Christ and the Spirit helps us begin to make sense of how we should approach the practice of theology. The discipline of theology proceeds rightly when it begins from the presupposition that all right thinking and speaking about God, reality and history takes its bearings from the life of the incarnate Jesus Christ. Our thinking about God has to follow after him, because our knowledge of God takes place in and through him. . . . This stands in line with Paul's statement that the Spirit shows us the "depths of God" by making us participants in the "mind of Christ" himself (1 Cor. 2:10–16). Our participation in Christ's mind is how our fallen minds are "renewed in knowledge according to the image of [our] creator" (Col. 3:10), and this is the precise renewal we need in order to think and speak about God rightly as theologians.[49]

48. Alan J. Torrance, "*Auditus Fidei*: Where and How Does God Speak? Faith, Reason, and the Question of Criteria," in *Reason and the Reasons of Faith*, ed. Paul J. Griffiths and Reinhard Hütter (New York: T&T Clark, 2005), 29, 36; Alan J. Torrance and Andrew B. Torrance, "Recovering the Person: The Crisis of Natural- ism and the Theological Insights of Søren Kierkegaard and Karl Barth," *Crux* 48, no. 3 (Fall 2012): 51–55.

49. Keith L. Johnson, *Theology as Discipleship* (Downers Grove, IL: IVP Aca- demic, 2015), 59–60.

Authentically *Christ-ian* theology is not for those who desire to remain spectators, those who have an armchair interest in Christ but decline the call of Christ to be formed in Christ. For contrary to the sophistic naivete of some, especially this side of the Enlightenment, the mystery of the Word made flesh cannot be known by the sort of detached deliberation that attempts to deconstruct or domesticate him from a distance. Jesus Christ is known in faith and discipleship or he is not known at all. Anything else is merely religious shadowboxing from which comes nothing of value and in which the Lord and *Logos* of Christian theology refuses to take part.[50] Our practice of theology proceeds rightly only from a life-giving, mind-renewing participation in the One who assures us, "I am the way, and the truth, and the life. No one comes to the Father except through me" (John 14:6).

If knowledge of God and access to God could be directly attained from the world or from ourselves, the mediation of Jesus Christ would be superfluous. Lack of clarity and conviction on this point only advances what Alexander Schmemann calls "the real cause of *secularism*, which is ultimately nothing else but the affirmation of the world's autonomy, of its self-sufficiency in terms of reason, knowledge, and action."[51] So let us decisively discard all notions of naturalistic and unmediated ways to God, since God the Son assures us that they do not exist. Jesus Christ, conceived in Mary's womb by the Spirit, is himself the Way to God, in whom alone the Father is known and accessed. Jesus being the Way to God affords Christian theology a datum point that is distinctly Christian and an order of inquiry that is properly theological. Our datum point is God in Christ, and all else in relation to Christ—never the world or ourselves according to our self-understanding, but always the *Logos* and all things according to his self-disclosure. Our order of inquiry thus begins with Christ and does not turn from Christ even when turning to nondivine things. For we are no less beholden to the mystery of God

50. Helmut Thielicke, *Out of the Depths*, trans. G. W. Bromiley (Grand Rapids: Eerdmans, 1962), 65–67.

51. Schmemann, *For the Life of the World*, 129 (emphasis original).

when beholding the works of God, in that the latter are not somehow more assessable and less demanding, subject to the mere free play of our natural human ability. As such, Christian theology serves as a standing rebuke of the world's autonomy and self-sufficiency, in that Jesus is the Way who unmasks the modern myth that there are aspects of human existence in which God can be evaded or from which God can be exiled.[52]

Given that God is not directly known and accessed *from* the world or ourselves, Christian theology is incompatible with *natural theology*—the notion that God can be merely discovered or conceived in unmediated fashion by our intuitive, experiential, and empirical observations of the natural order. But it is nevertheless true that God is known and accessed *in* the world through Jesus, such that Christian theology has a robust *theology of nature*—a rich doctrine of creation and theological perspective on the world. Natural theology and a Christian theology of nature are different from top to bottom, and the differences are both stark and momentous. Yet the primary issue is whether Jesus actually is, as he assures us, the Way and the Truth, the one true logic and criterion of all truth. Karl Barth notes, "When man has tried to read the truth from sun, moon and stars or from himself, the result has been an idol. But when God has been known and then known again in the world, so that the result was a joyful praise of God in creation, that is because he is to be sought and found by us in Jesus Christ."[53] When God is not sought in Christ, God is found nowhere. But when God is found in Christ, creation is revealed for what it truly is: the theater where all things great and small, extraordinary and mundane, reflect God's glory. In other words, the *Logos* gives Christian theology a distinct logic and unitary frame of

52. John Webster, "What Makes Theology Theological?," *Journal of Analytic Theology* 3 (May 2015): 17–19. As Dietrich Bonhoeffer so wisely insisted, "Theological thought goes from God to reality, not from reality to God." *Act and Being*, ed. Wayne Whitson Floyd Jr., trans. H. Martin Rumscheidt, vol. 2 of *Dietrich Bonhoeffer Works*, ed. Wayne Whitson Floyd Jr. (Minneapolis: Fortress, 1996), 89.

53. Karl Barth, *Dogmatics in Outline*, trans. G. T. Thomson (New York: Harper & Row, 1959), 52.

knowing.[54] The church may thus live, move, and have its being rapt in the Truth who is Christ, assured not only of the meaning of its existence but also of the ground and goal of the world. For Jesus is himself the Truth—not one truth among others, but the Truth that creates and renders intelligible all other truth, because he is the Truth of God, the first and ultimate Truth in heaven and on earth.[55]

Even more, Jesus assures us that he is the Life, come to grant us a share in the very life of God in and through himself. He proclaims, "This is eternal life, that they know you, the only true God, and Jesus Christ whom you have sent" (John 17:3). The condition for theological knowing, then, is not that of entitlement or achievement. Rather, the condition is participation in the eternal life given as sheer, extravagant gift in Christ—that grand and glorious life that the Father, Son, and Spirit have together enjoyed from before the creation of time itself.[56] The faith once and for all delivered to the saints really is the most exciting, imagination-staggering drama the world shall ever know. Jesus Christ is the epicenter of the action, and amid the tempest and tumult of the world, he asks his beloved church this all-important, all-encompassing question: Who do *you* say that I am? Let us be sure that our answer rings with an awed and astonished affirmation that he is the Lord and *Logos* of Christian theology.

54. Torrance, "*Auditus Fidei*: Where and How Does God Speak?," 50–52.
55. Barth, *Dogmatics in Outline*, 26; Donald Bloesch, *The Ground of Certainty: Toward an Evangelical Theology of Revelation* (Grand Rapids: Eerdmans, 1971), 126–28, 135–39.
56. Rae, "Prolegomena," 16.

Father, Son, and Holy Spirit

The Triune Shape of Christian Theology

Jesus Christ is the Word of God made flesh, the glorious and defining expression of God's revelation to humanity. He is the reality of God and the reality of humankind in one resplendent personal being. That is why he was, is, and shall evermore remain the Lord and *Logos* of all Christian thought. However, Jesus is that Lord, and that Word, only and ever because he is the Son of God. The apostle Peter's answer to Jesus's heart-piercing question—"Who do you say that I am?"—became the fulcrum for Christian theology ever since: "You are the Christ, *the Son of the living God*." We can sense the delight in Jesus's reaction: "Blessed are you, Simon Bar-Jonah! For flesh and blood has not revealed this to you, but my Father who is in heaven" (Matt. 16:15–17). Peter may have had a lot to learn, but his divinely enabled utterance was a revelation of the most basic truth about Jesus Christ: he is Son to a heavenly Father. What Jesus tirelessly impressed on Peter and his fellow disciples was that Jesus could be truly known only in relation to his Father and that this sublime knowledge could only come through the ministry of the Holy Spirit (e.g., John 14:15–21). The reality that Christ opened to the world is

thus entirely three-dimensional. The truth of the Word made flesh
is the truth that this Word is the eternal Son of the Father in the fellowship of the Spirit. The revelation of Christ was not, is not, and
cannot be other than the revelation of the beauty of the Holy Trinity. To honor Christ is to honor the Father and the Spirit. To believe
in Christ is to believe that he has been sent by the Father through
the Spirit. To know the truth of God and the world in Christ is to
know that he is the ever-beloved Son of the Father by the illumina-
tion and inner witness of the Spirit. In sum, to experience Christ is
to experience the all-encompassing, reality-altering truth of God
the Holy Trinity.

The eternal life and love of God is the life and love the Father has
for the Son in the Spirit, which has no beginning as surely as it has
no end. It is this life, this love, this *reality*, that Jesus brought among
us and in us. God the Son was sent—indeed, it was his principal
mission from the Father—to bring the endless joy and ecstasy, the
eternal freedom and holiness, the everlasting pleasure and peace of
God's triune existence into the world as a gift. Simply stated, only
overtly trinitarian theology is overtly Christian theology.

The Reality of the Trinity and the Trinity as Reality

G. K. Chesterton quipped, "People have fallen into a foolish habit
of speaking of orthodoxy as something heavy, humdrum, and safe."
Quite the contrary: "There never was anything so perilous or so exciting as orthodoxy."[1] We ought not assume that the "people" to whom
Chesterton refers are scoffing, cultured despisers of Christianity.
Indeed, it is all too common for Christians themselves to exhibit a
kind of apathetic indifference toward, or even grudging acceptance
of, orthodoxy ("right doctrine") as something to be endured rather
than something to be enjoyed. Even among otherwise faithful believers, doctrine is rarely viewed as "perilous" or "exciting." It is seen as

1. G. K. Chesterton, *Orthodoxy* (Colorado Springs: Shaw, 2001), 148–49.

important and necessary, perhaps, but hardly dangerous or invigorating. We already dealt with a number of factors that account for this case of theological dissonance, which we need not rehearse here. We need only emphasize Chesterton's point: it is foolish to speak of doctrine as humdrum and safe. This is not to say that orthodoxy cannot be *taught* in such a way as to invite boredom or that orthodoxy may not be *received* with the boredom that marks boring people—but, in either case, the label "foolish" still applies. And it is all the more foolish when the doctrine at hand is the Trinity, for here the church articulates the essential truth about God, who is as fascinating as he is fearsome. If the church is to recover the proper place of theological formation at the heart of Christian doctrine, we must grasp that doctrine is *transparent*; that is, we must relearn that theology serves its divinely intended purpose only when we look *through* what it teaches to the realities it articulates. After all, that is doctrine's divine intent: to describe a perilous and exciting reality. Wherever theology becomes opaque and thus self-referential—when theology seeks to exist for its own sake rather than for the sake of knowing the triune God—it necessarily becomes pedantic and abstract. Soon enough it becomes out of touch and tune with the worship of the saints.

Any attempt to imagine and describe reality, as we have shown, must begin and end with Jesus Christ. And because it begins and ends with him, our descriptions of reality necessarily involve the invocation of his Father and the Spirit. The incarnation of God is God's definitive self-revelation, such that in Christ Jesus we are taught to confess reality in terms of the Trinity. All our theology, and thus all our life, is to be oriented to the one grand and glorious truth of God. In Christ we encounter God, and the God we encounter in Christ is always the Holy Trinity. That is why, as Thomas F. Torrance powerfully puts it, the doctrines of the incarnation and the Trinity are necessarily bound together:

> The doctrines of the Trinity and of the incarnation thus form together the nucleus at the heart of the Christian conception of God and

constitute the ontological and epistemological basis for the formulation of every Christian doctrine. . . . It is not just that the doctrine of the Holy Trinity must be accorded primacy over all the other doctrines, but that properly understood it is the nerve and centre of them all, configures them all, and is so deeply integrated with them that when they are held apart from the doctrine of the Trinity they are seriously defective in truth and become malformed.[2]

If theology is an articulation of God, then surely it seeks what is most real. As an articulation of that reality, theology is necessarily defined by God: If God is the Reality, then reality is the Trinity. And the Trinity, Fred Sanders has written so well, "changes everything."[3] The thesis of this book is that theology shapes our understanding of reality. It can do so only when it truthfully and accurately confesses the life, love, beauty, and joy that has characterized the church's experience of God from the very beginning. Michael Reeves is right: the deepest meaning of our lives depends on the existence of the Trinity. "Indeed, in the triune God is the love behind all love, the life behind all life, the music behind all music, the beauty behind all beauty and the joy behind all joy."[4]

Can Reeves be taken seriously? After all, if he is right, then the brightness of God's three-personal existence sheds light on the most profound experiences of human life. And if Reeves is right, then no enlightenment whatsoever can be gained from Immanuel Kant's blithe assertion that "absolutely *nothing can be acquired for practical life* from the doctrine of the Trinity."[5] In fact it is patently absurd. We are tempted to conclude that Kant had yet to read the New Testa-

2. Thomas F. Torrance, *The Christian Doctrine of God: One Being Three Persons* (London: T&T Clark, 1996), 30–31.

3. Fred Sanders, *The Deep Things of God: How the Trinity Changes Everything* (Wheaton: Crossway, 2010).

4. Michael Reeves, *Delighting in the Trinity: An Introduction to the Christian Faith* (Downers Grove, IL: IVP Academic, 2012), 62.

5. Immanuel Kant, *"Der Streit der Fakultäten,"* in *Werke in sechs Bänden*, ed. W. Weischedel (Darmstadt: Wissenschaftliche Buchgesellschaft, 1964), 50 (emphasis original), quoted in Miroslav Volf, "The Trinity and the Church," in *Trinitarian*

ment with any depth, engage the history of the church with any real humility—or to have "tasted and seen" of God in any significant way. It is precisely the knowledge of God *as Trinity* that altered forever the way Christians have understood life in its deepest dimensions. The doctrine of the Trinity is not a speculative supplement to a generic doctrine of God that is already sufficient to account for reality and its "practical" dimensions. Quite the opposite. The Trinity is the only sufficient ground for that reality. If the doctrine of the Trinity has nothing substantive to say about our "practical life" (if we must speak this way), then the difference between Trinity and idolatry is negligible—any old theology will do. But such thinking would remove us very far from Holy Scripture, where we encounter the blood-bought conviction that Father, Son, and Spirit mark the difference between reality and its counterfeits. If God is the bedrock of all that is true and real, then true and real understanding of God is paramount. If "practicality" is an implication of what is ultimately true and real, then to say that the Trinity has no such implication for Christian life is simply to slip into an unreal truthfulness or an untruthful reality—an utter absurdity either way. If it is "practical" to think, speak, and act in accordance with reality, then the Trinity is the basic condition for the "practical life."

"When I Say 'God,' I Mean Father, Son, and Holy Ghost"

These words belong to Gregory of Nazianzus, the great fourth-century archbishop of Constantinople.[6] They were critically important in his own day, full of the necessary precision employed to combat the Arian heresy, which sought to compromise the extraordinarily good news that Jesus Christ is none other than God incarnate. We must ask whether the semantic precision and conviction exhibited by Gregory is not equally important and necessary in our own day, when

---

Soundings in Systematic Theology, ed. Paul Louis Metzger (London: T&T Clark, 2006), 159.

　6. Gregory of Nazianzus, *Orations*, no. 38.8, in *NPNF²*, 7:347.

the doctrine of the Trinity is so often viewed as esoteric, pedantic, or impractical—even by those within the church. What difference does it make if we mean "Father, Son, and Holy Spirit" when we say "God"? The question is especially relevant when talk about God only seems problematized by our confession of his threefold essence, frequently objected to on the grounds that it can be an unnecessary hindrance to "authentic piety," or perhaps a stumbling block to "religious ecumenism." In either case, the implication is that what we mean when we say "God" exists merely on the periphery of an understanding of God, which is apparently capable of sustaining Christian life and witness apart from who God actually is. If the life and witness of the church can indeed be sustained apart from a settled, joyful conviction that God is Holy Trinity, then Kant becomes prophetic and Gregory of Nazianzus merely archaic.

When the church is awake and alert, it is Gregorian rather than Kantian, recognizing that what we mean when we say "God" defines and determines our nature, worship, and mission. The doctrine of the Trinity is no mere "take" on God, a mere mental construct derived from our speculative musings about god-in-the-abstract. It is an articulation of a divine encounter that shakes reality to the core, turning upside-down things right side up again. Thomas F. Torrance wisely notes that the revelation of God as Father, Son, and Spirit

> is a mystery so utterly strange and so radically different that it cannot be apprehended and substantiated except out of itself, and even then it infinitely exceeds what we are ever able to conceive or spell out. Far less may it be assimilated into man's familiar world of meaning and be brought into line with the framework of its commonly accepted truths, for the radically new conception of God proclaimed in the Gospel calls for a complete transformation of man's outlook in terms of a new divine order which cannot be derived from or inferred from anything conceived by man before. In point of fact it actually conflicts sharply with generally accepted beliefs and established ideas in human culture and initiates a seismic reconstruction not only of

religious and intellectual belief but of the very foundation of human life and knowledge.[7]

According to Torrance, the revelation of the gospel entails a revolutionary upheaval of human thought based on a conflict with, and reconstruction of, the foundation of human life and knowledge. If he is right that the *foundation* of human knowledge and life is transformed by the revelation of God as Trinity, then we are a very long way from Kant's heedless indifference to the seismic implications of God's self-revelation. But, even so and all the better, we are all the closer to the Word of God, in whom conflict (death) and reconstruction (resurrection) lead to a transformation (renewal) of our minds and life (Rom. 12:1–2). The gift of God the Father, through the Holy Spirit, is that we may share the mind of Christ (1 Cor. 2:12–16). When we are crucified with him, resurrected with him, and made forever new in him, our human knowing and living is elevated into the reality of God the Father through the Spirit. When that happens, we can never be who we once were.

Applied to our knowledge of God, Dietrich Bonhoeffer's assertion that "all concepts of reality that ignore Jesus Christ are abstractions" is especially poignant.[8] Above all other concepts of reality, any concept of God that does not necessitate our sharing in Christ's knowledge of his Father through the Spirit is hopelessly abstract, a movement away from what is real. Such a movement has been a perennial temptation in the church, perhaps especially in the Western church, where the doctrine of the Trinity has from time to time been relativized and attenuated—held in abeyance—by a doctrine of God that is articulated (or "defended") apart from God's essential triune nature.[9] What is implied in such a theological move is that God can

7. Torrance, *Christian Doctrine of God*, 19.
8. Dietrich Bonhoeffer, *Ethics*, ed. Clifford J. Green, trans. Reinhard Krauss et al., vol. 6 of *Dietrich Bonhoeffer Works*, ed. Wayne Whitson Floyd Jr. and Victoria J. Barnett (Minneapolis: Fortress, 2005), 54.
9. Robert Letham, *The Holy Trinity: In Scripture, History, Theology, and Worship* (Phillipsburg, NJ: P&R, 2004), 4.

be known and inferred apart from his self-disclosure in Jesus Christ by the Spirit—that an answer to the question, Who is God? can be given apart from an answer to the question from our Lord: "Who do you say that I am?" If knowledge of God can be apprehended apart from Jesus, then we must not feign surprise when the doctrine of the Trinity is pushed to the theological margins, becoming a "problem" needing a solution or apology, or even becoming an object of consternation among the faithful rather than a source of unmitigated joy and wonder.

Gregory's dictum—"When I say 'God,' I mean Father, Son, and Holy Ghost"—found an echo in Athanasius, his contemporary. The fourth-century bishop of Alexandria and fellow combatant in the church's battle against Arianism wrote, "It is more pious and more accurate to signify God from the Son and call Him Father, than to name Him from His works only and call Him Unoriginate."[10] Both Gregory and Athanasius knew that Christian confession of God must derive from who God really is, that God must be named and known from within his self-giving and self-revelation in Christ. Therefore, a philosophically derived, generic theism is a woefully deficient and untenable understanding of God. The church's confession, prayer, and proclamation that God is Holy Trinity does not originate as an implication of a doctrine of God previously constructed, as if "Trinity" fills out a prior conception of "God" that we already possessed. Torrance is right: the doctrine of the Trinity calls for "the rejection even of theism as quite inadequate and theologically unacceptable. . . . To admit any other than a trinitarian way of thinking about God is in fact not only to relativise and question the truth of the Trinity but to contradict the Trinity and to set aside the Gospel."[11]

The life, existence, and delight of the church—the gospel that is her breath and song—is that our heavenly Father has given us his Son so that in him, by the power and presence of the Spirit, we may have forgiveness, healing, reconciliation, redemption, and thus everlasting

10. Athanasius, *Against the Arians* 1.33–34, in *NPNF*[2], 4:326.
11. Torrance, *Christian Doctrine of God*, 24.

life in the communion of our triune God. It is precisely *who* God is that defines *how* God is for us; and is it precisely *who* and *how* God is that gives shape, substance, and meaning to our lives. John Calvin's insistence that "the chief good of man is nothing else but union with God"[12] was echoed a century later in the very first question of the Westminster Catechism: "What is the chief and highest end of man?" The answer is revealing: "Man's chief and highest end is to glorify God, and fully to enjoy him forever." To this we might add: if God is not the blessed and Holy Trinity, then not only is it not *possible* to glorify and enjoy communion with him forever, it is not *worth* it. Jesus is the Way, Truth, and Life of his Father, and thus the chief good and highest end of human destiny. Vladimir Lossky does not exaggerate when he writes, "If we reject the Trinity as the sole ground of all reality and of all thought, we are committed to a road that leads nowhere; we end in an aporia, in folly, in the disintegration of our being, in spiritual death. Between the Trinity and hell there lies no other choice. This question is, indeed, crucial—in the literal sense of that word. The dogma of the Trinity is a cross for human ways of thought."[13]

The dogma of the Trinity is indeed the sole ground of all reality and thought, because God is nothing less or other than the meaning of all that exists; it cannot be otherwise, because God cannot be other than who he is. To know and confess God in some other way than as Father, Son, and Spirit commits one to despair, foolishness, and death. Why? Because God is the truth, wisdom, and life of the world—and it is his triune being alone that makes him so. But the Trinity, Lossky notes, is also a *cross* for human thought. Again, we may ask: Why? Because the way to the Father goes through Christ Jesus, whose revelation of the Father necessarily went through Golgotha, where he crucified our self-generated conceptions of God—our mythologies, idolatries, and

12. John Calvin, *Calvin's Commentaries*, Calvin Translation Society (Edinburgh: 1844–56; reprinted in 22 vols., Grand Rapids: Baker Books, 2003), 22:98, on Heb. 4:10.

13. Vladimir Lossky, *The Mystical Theology of the Eastern Church* (1957; repr., Cambridge: Clarke, 1973), 66.

specious speculations. This means a painful end to our rogue religiosity, a reorientation through death and resurrection to a mortified and vivified experience of the reality of God as God really is. The doctrine of the Trinity is not an invention of the church; it is the expression of a divine experience that birthed the church into existence in the first place. The theology of Christ's church is thoroughly trinitarian because we can know Christ only in the power of the Spirit, and the Christ we know is the Son of the Father. The Holy Trinity is not a theological speculation but the joyful and worshipful ground of our very existence.

The Trinitarian Shape of Christian Life, Joy, and Worship

When God the Son came to make his Father known, he did so through the power and presence of the Holy Spirit, and the people of God have never been the same. In and through Christ Jesus, the church's doctrine and doxology, praise and prayer, worship and witness, became and have remained melodiously trinitarian. Jesus himself taught the church to sing in a trinitarian key. In each and every instance where his apostles declare the name of the Father, Son, and Holy Spirit, that declaration is set to the tune of praise, adoration, wonder, mystery, and joy. There are no exceptions. The revelation of the triune God in Scripture is always very good news, and it is always reality altering. Many modern Christians might find this assertion rather surprising, owing perhaps to their particular experience of a "doctrinaire" trinitarianism, couched as it often is in dry, pedantic, and even apologetically tortured treatments that are out of touch and tune with the doxological exclamations of the apostles and their Savior.

What does it mean to say that Jesus taught the church to sing in a trinitarian key? It means that Jesus's revelation of his Father through the Spirit brought his disciples, then and now, into a life-transforming experience that elicited their praise and worship. It means that the church's heart became indelibly impressed with the glory, wonder, and joy of a three-personal God. It means that the apostles, who testified to this reality throughout the New Testament, were doing more than merely "doctrinal instruction." They were singing that doctrine, rejoicing as they wrote about the incomparable joy of experiencing God in Christ Jesus. We do a *massive* hermeneutical disservice to the testimony of the apostles if we read their words as flat and mono-tone. After all, their testimony is filled with praise and prayer as they exalt the Father and the Son in the power of the Spirit. "Blessed be the God and Father of our Lord Jesus Christ!" Peter declares (1 Pet. 1:3). "Grace, mercy, and peace will be with us, from God the Father and from Jesus Christ the Father's Son, in truth and love," exclaims John (2 John 3). "Blessed be the God and Father of our Lord Jesus Christ," Paul proclaims, "who has blessed us in Christ with every spiritual blessing in the heavenly places" (Eph. 1:3). The experience of God's triune grace, love, and fellowship has provided the church with the holy and jubilant benediction that has marked its worship ever since: "The grace of the Lord Jesus Christ and the love of God and the fellowship of the Holy Spirit be with you all" (2 Cor. 13:14).

The exuberance we encounter in the apostolic testimony is won-derful, yet it is little wonder that we find such exuberance. The re-peated, rhapsodic testimony of the apostles is the fulfillment of a promise given to them by our Lord, a promise that exceeded their wildest expectations: "And I will ask the Father, and he will give you another Helper, to be with you forever, even the Spirit of truth. . . . I will not leave you as orphans; I will come to you. . . . In that day you will know that I am in my Father, and you in me, and I in you" (John 14:16–20). Very shortly thereafter, Jesus repeats this jaw-dropping, heart-stopping promise when he prays to his Father:

> I do not ask for [the disciples] only, but also for those who will believe in me through their word, that they may all be one, just as you, Father, are in me, and I in you. . . . The glory that you have given me I have given to them, that they may be one even as we are one, I in them and you in me. . . . I made known to them your name, and I will continue to make it known, that the love with which you have loved me may be in them, and I in them. (John 17:20–26)

D. A. Carson notes that in this prayer we are confronted with a promise so remarkable as to be "breathtakingly extravagant."[14] And if any promise could be extravagant enough to take our breath away, surely it is this one! For the promise entails and ensures that, through the Holy Spirit, Christ will be in us and we will be in Christ in such a way that we come to share in the eternal life, love, and unity the Father has with the Son. As unsurpassably wonderful as it is, it is again no wonder that Jesus says "And this is eternal life, that they know you, the only true God, and Jesus Christ whom you have sent" (John 17:3). Strange as it may sound to our modern ears, Jesus equates knowing God with eternal life. How can knowing God and eternal life be synonymous? Because knowing God *in Christ* means experiencing the life that Jesus has eternally known with his Father in the Spirit. The triune life of God is the eternal life of which Jesus speaks, because it is the only life which "wert and art and evermore shalt be"![15] The miraculous gift of our Lord Jesus is that all who believe in him shall be partakers in the life of the Trinity.[16]

The apostles experienced the miracle of knowing God as Father, Son, and Spirit, and they put that experience to melodious words. They attuned their minds and hearts to the revelation given them by Jesus, and what they recalled and reported remains indecipherable apart from their experience of coming to know the never-ceasing joy and boundless life they found with the Father, in Jesus Christ, through the communion of the Spirit. The witness of the apostles is a testament to the incarnate mission of the Son of God, which we may put as concisely as possible: to make his Father known in the Spirit. In all that Jesus proclaimed as the living embodiment of the good news—whether forgiveness, peace, love, mercy, righteousness,

14. D. A. Carson, *The Gospel according to John*, Pillar New Testament Commentary (Grand Rapids: Eerdmans, 1991), 569.

15. Reginald Heber, "Holy, Holy, Holy! Lord God Almighty," *Hymns for the Family of God* (Nashville: Brentwood-Benson, 1976), no. 323.

16. On this point it is difficult to improve upon Donald Fairbairn, *Life in the Trinity: An Introduction to Theology with the Help of the Church Fathers* (Downers Grove, IL: IVP Academic, 2009).

kingdom, heaven, life, or truth—the singular design and purpose in it all was to bring humanity to experience the unfathomable depths of his Father's love through the Spirit. Who Jesus is and what Jesus did cannot be apprehended apart from this decisive and definitive truth. Through his conception and birth, by his baptism and life, in his death, resurrection, and ascension, Jesus became in our humanity the living Way to his Father through the Spirit. This, he knew above all things, was the highest possible blessing, the kind of blessing that would re-create the cosmos, bringing it into new and unending life. Here is a life that brought everything and everyone into existence from the beginning, a life that would now elevate that existence into the thrice-holy euphoric love of the one eternal God.

Jesus is the eternal life he gives, and that life is the glorious experience of knowing his Father. "Father, the hour has come; glorify your Son that the Son may glorify you, since you have given him authority over all flesh, to give eternal life to all whom you have given him. And this is eternal life, *that they know you*, the only true God, and Jesus Christ whom you have sent" (John 17:1–3). The eternal life that Jesus Christ secures for us, in all that he is and does, is the life of God within our humanity. The New Testament was born from this experience, and so was the historic confession of the church. Following the apostles, and through their testimony to the Word made flesh, the church came to know the same life-giving and reality-altering truth of the triune God. Like the apostles, this reality came to shape all that the church said and sung. This was a reality so precious and so utterly and fundamentally sacred that Christians have ever since declared it essential to Christian existence: "We believe in God the Father Almighty. . . . We believe in Jesus Christ his Son, our Lord. . . . We believe in the Holy Spirit."[17]

17. "The Apostles' Creed (c. 400)," in CC, 25. Phillip Cary is exactly right: "If you want to know what Christian theology really means by the word 'God,' therefore, you have to direct your attention in worship to the Father, the Son, and the Holy Spirit. You can't really say what Christians believe in without using some version of that three-fold name, as is done throughout Christian worship as well as in the Creed." *The Meaning of Protestant Theology: Luther, Augustine, and the Gospel that Gives Us Christ* (Grand Rapids: Baker Academic, 2019), 308.

How easy it would be for us to forget, in our sometimes lazy and apathetic recitations of the Apostles' Creed, that what we confess is in fact a confession of the most blessed and sublime truth that has ever been and will ever be. The church has always known to require subscription to these words from all who profess the name of Christ. It is a requirement, we must insist, born not from a joyless desire to enforce "doctrinal orthodoxy" but rather to enshrine forever in the minds and hearts of Christians the most basic of all truths: God is our Father, in and through the Lord Jesus, by and through the Holy Spirit. This confession, above all others, is the heart and soul, the ground and grammar, of all Christian life, joy, and witness. Without confessing God as triune, we have nothing to confess that really matters—no joy, assurance, conviction, or worship worth having; indeed, no gospel and no Jesus worth clinging to.

The one, holy, catholic, apostolic church became the recipient of the melodious mystery of the Trinity and, mesmerized by the implications, gave them voice. The church, at its catholic and evangelical best, recognized that the truth of God's tri-unity is the luminous lynchpin of any and all authentic Christian belief. "The mystery of the Most Holy Trinity is the central mystery of Christian faith and life. It is the mystery of God in himself. It is therefore the source of all the other mysteries of faith, the light that enlightens them. It is the most fundamental and essential teaching in the 'hierarchy of the truths of faith.'"[18] We might be sympathetic to the common Christian for whom a statement of this sort sounds a tad hyperbolic, assaulted as she is with defensive and nervous explanations and solutions to the "problem of the Trinity." Yet once we are permitted to dispense with the jejune and artificial attempts to empty the Trinity of mystery—through analogies that employ eggs, clover leaves, or H_2O—we may embrace again the fundamental and essential place the Holy Trinity has in our common confession. We are then in a much better position

---

18. "The Profession of the Christian Faith," in *Catechism of the Catholic Church*, 2nd ed. (Vatican: Libreria Editrice Vaticana, 1994), 62.

to join the church in her doctrinal doxologies, expressing the beautiful mystery that lies at the heart of her eternal comfort.

We could hardly do better than to join Martin Luther, who expounded the Apostles' Creed thus: "For in all three articles God himself has revealed and opened to us the most profound depths of his fatherly heart and his pure, unutterable love. For this very purpose he created us, so that he might redeem us and make us holy, and, moreover, having granted and bestowed upon us everything in heaven and on earth, he has also given us his Son and his Holy Spirit, through whom he brings us to himself."[19] It is difficult to read these words without hearing an echo of the apostles themselves, who took similar joy from their experience of the Father's pure and unfathomable love in Christ. Our common confession that God is Father, Son, and Spirit is a confession that spans creation and redemption—the sort of declaration that frames reality. From beginning to end, the hope and happiness of all Christians that God not only creates us but also seeks to make us forever his is grounded in God's tri-unity.

Especially worth noting is that Luther's words come from his Large Catechism. The words of a catechism are meant to be rehearsed and memorized and, more to the point, *cherished* by all who come to faith in Christ. Such words are designed to become the vocabulary through which Christians understand God, the world, and themselves. When it comes time to confess what really matters, what reality ultimately consists of, what brings us the greatest joy and comfort, we confess together that God is holy and loving Trinity.

The Heidelberg Catechism is another exemplary instance of this insistence by Christians. The very first question and answer are composed in an inescapably, indispensably trinitarian key:

1. *What is your only comfort in life and in death?*
    That I, with body and soul, both in life and in death (Rom. 14:7–8), am not my own (1 Cor. 6:19), but belong to my faithful Savior Jesus

19. Martin Luther, "The Large Catechism (1529)," in *BC*, 439.

Christ (1 Cor. 3:23), who with His precious blood (1 Peter 1:18–19) has fully satisfied for all my sins (1 John 1:7; 1 John 2:2), and redeemed me from all the power of the devil (1 John 3:8); and so preserves me (John 6:39) that without the will of my Father in heaven not a hair can fall away from my head (Matt. 10:29–30; Luke 21:18); indeed, that all things must work together for my salvation (Rom. 8:28). Wherefore, by His Holy Spirit, He also assures me of eternal life (2 Cor. 1:21–22; Eph. 1:13–14; Rom. 8:16), and makes me heartily willing and ready from now on to live unto Him (Rom. 8:1).[20]

Whether in life or death, the only true comfort of the Christian is that God is Trinity. And because God is exactly who he is as Father, Son, and Spirit, God is and remains the source of the Christian's deepest delight and determination.

The manifold expressions of this delight permeate the witness of the church from age to age, constituting a crescendo of praise that puts to permanent flight the notion that the doctrine of the Trinity exists at the speculative margins of Christian faith. It is difficult to improve on the words of the French Protestant preacher Adolphe Monod (1802–56) on this most salient of points:

> The relation of the Father, the Son and the Holy Spirit to man corresponds to a relationship in God between the Father, the Son and the Holy Spirit; and the love which is poured out to save us is the expression of that love which has dwelt eternally in the bosom of God. Ah! The doctrine then becomes for us so touching and profound! There we find the basis of the Gospel, and those who reject it as a speculative and purely theological doctrine have therefore never understood the least thing about it; it is the strength of our hearts, it is the joy of our souls, it is the life of our life, it is the very foundation of revealed truth.[21]

20. *The Heidelberg Catechism (1563)*, in *Reformed Confessions of the 16th and 17th Centuries in English Translation*, vol. 2, *1552–1566*, comp. James T. Dennison Jr. (Grand Rapids: Reformation Heritage Books, 2010), 771.

21. Adolphe Monod, *Adolphe Monod's Farewell to His Friends and to His Church*, trans. Owen Thomas (London: Banner of Truth, 1962), 114, quoted in Sanders, *The Deep Things of God*, 166.

We ought to take these words as a summative, even normative, expression of the deepest and most profound experience of God's beloved children. For it is in the inner and essential nature of God's existence as Trinity that Christians find the strength, joy, life, and foundation of their own existence. To confess that God is Father, Son, and Spirit is to confess the truth: the truth of God, the truth of ourselves, and the truth of all the world besides. Theology can never be less, or other, than a confession of that truth.

All Things Exist Because God Is Holy Trinity

When we begin with the Father, Son, and Spirit, we are able to discern the foundation of all things, including the most important: "In the beginning, God created the heavens and the earth" (Gen. 1:1). There is perhaps no phrase in literary history more repeated, and reflected on, than this one—even among those who are suspicious as to its truthfulness. It has achieved a kind of canonical status in Western literature, owing in large part to its existence as the first sentence of perhaps the most influential book in all of human history. This sentence has become literarily sacrosanct, commonly acknowledged as a true statement about the genesis of the universe—about how anything and anyone came into being—by nearly all who believe in a divine being. The most significant of those who revered, reflected on, and then repeated this phrase was the apostle John. By virtue of his encounter with the Lord Jesus, John saw fit to generate a new Genesis, a seismic, apostolic reinterpretation of the first book of the Bible: "In the beginning was the Word, and the Word was with God, and the Word was God. He was in the beginning with God. All things were made through him, and without him was not any thing made that was made" (John 1:1–3). The allusion to the first Genesis is supposed to be obvious—"In the beginning"—but what follows from John's divinely inspired testimony is anything but. In concert with his fellow apostles, John changed forever the way Christians understand creation. Most assuredly, God spoke creation into existence "out of nothing" (Latin, *ex nihilo*), but not *through* nothing. The Word through which God spoke the cosmos into existence out of nothing is his Son, his beloved Son. Otherwise, nothing would exist.

The apostle Paul encountered the very same Word—the Word become flesh—and had the same reaction as John. Paul, too, would never read the book of Genesis in the same way again: "[The Son] is the image of the invisible God, the firstborn of all creation. For by him all things were created, in heaven and on earth, visible and invisible, whether thrones or dominions or rulers or authorities—all things were created through him and for him. And he is before all things, and in him all things hold together" (Col. 1:15–17).[22] Let us not miss the import of this. Saul the Pharisee would have gladly affirmed that God created heaven and earth, but when Saul meets Jesus and is born again as the apostle Paul, he all the more gladly restates the reality: God created all things in heaven and earth *in, through, and for Christ.* That God created the world may be admitted by all "theists," but how and why God created the world can only be known in Christ. The origin, design, purpose, and *telos* of creation are only truthfully confessed in a trinitarian key, for creation depends on a God who has a Son and is a life-giving Spirit. God the Father created everything in heaven and earth for his Son and through his Son, by the inspiration and fellowship of the Spirit. The witness of the apostles leads us to a remarkable and even startling conclusion: God the Father created the cosmos as a gift, a gift he bestows on his Son—by and through his Son (Col. 1:16). The creation of the world, in other words, is born out of the everlasting love the Father has for his Son in the communion of the Spirit. The existence of the universe is thus a testimony to the

22. This passage led David Fergusson to provocatively exclaim, "The world was made so that Christ might be born." "Creation," in *The Oxford Handbook of Systematic Theology*, ed. John Webster, Kathryn Tanner, and Iain Torrance (New York: Oxford University Press, 2007), 77. Fergusson's provocation sounds a bit extravagant for those accustomed to conceive of the incarnation of the Word as an emergency measure for the fall of humanity. We would do well to reconsider this customary conception, considering that the apostle Paul ascribes the creation of all things to Jesus the incarnate Redeemer.

eternal life and love of the Trinity; the world we inhabit throbs with the joy and music of God's interpersonal intimacy.

In recognition of this astounding reality, Christians have learned to say and sing in unison: "We believe in one God, the Father, the Almighty, *maker of heaven and earth.* . . . We believe in one Lord, Jesus Christ. . . . *Through him all things were made.* . . . We believe in the Holy Spirit, the Lord, the *giver of life.*"[23] The Nicene Creed, in obedience to Holy Scripture, frames a Christian confession of creation in a very specific trinitarian way, allowing the church not only to profess and delight in God's purpose for the world but also to forestall the temptation to conceive of creation in some way that is not according to God's inner being and life. The doctrine of the Trinity is no more an addendum to a preconceived doctrine of creation than is the Trinity an addendum to a preconceived doctrine of God. Our doctrine of creation is every bit as trinitarian as our doctrine of God; we believe that God created all things in heaven and earth, in other words, exactly *because* we believe God is Father, Son, and Spirit. Just as God only exists because God is Trinity, so too creation only exists because God is Trinity. No Trinity, no God; no Trinity, no creation.

The church bears witness to the eternal fecundity of God when we say that the Son is eternally begotten and the Spirit eternally proceeds from the Father. God's inner being is eternally generative, and because God is eternal triune life in himself, he is well pleased to create life outside of himself—the universe exists as a created echo of a reality in the Creator. "If God were not triune," Herman Bavinck rightly asserts, "creation would not be possible."[24] The creation of the heavens and the earth is an expression not of God's boredom, loneliness, neediness, or paucity but of his interpersonal intimacy and delight. Creation happens because the Father delights in his

23. "The Nicene Creed," in *The Book of Common Prayer* (New York: Oxford University Press, 1979), 326–27 (emphasis added).

24. Herman Bavinck, *In the Beginning: Foundations of Christian Theology*, ed. John Bolt, trans. John Vriend (Grand Rapids: Baker, 1999), 39.

Son and wills for that delight to be multiplied and magnified. That anything besides God exists at all is a testament to God's desire to share his delight. Jonathan Edwards has beautifully imagined this triune truth:

> Christ has brought it to pass, that those who the Father has given to him should be brought into the household of God, that he and his Father and they should be as it were one society, one family; that his people should be in a sort admitted into that society of the three persons in the Godhead. In this family or household God [is] the Father, Jesus Christ is his own naturally and eternally begotten Son. The saints, they also are children in the family; the church is the daughter of God, being the spouse of his Son. They all have communion in the same Spirit, the Holy Ghost.[25]

Edwards elsewhere put it in yet another, equally beautiful way: "The end of the creation of God was to provide a spouse for his Son Jesus Christ that might enjoy him and on whom he might pour forth his love."[26] Creation exists, and the reason it exists is to creatively magnify the Father's love for the Son in the Spirit—the world would not, and could not, exist otherwise.

C. S. Lewis imagined a similar beauty when, in *The Magician's Nephew*, he has the Christ figure, Aslan, *singing* Narnia into existence. Perhaps Lewis would agree that "Aslan" sings from a joy he has everlastingly known and experienced, from a love and harmony that could never be anything but the heavenly, melodious love of the Trinity. "Creation," writes Michael Reeves, "is about the spreading, the diffusion, the outward explosion of that love."[27] Therefore, to recall Gregory of Nazianzus, when Christians say God is Creator, we mean

25. Jonathan Edwards, *Miscellanies*, no. 571, in *The Works of Jonathan Edwards*, ed. Ava Chamberlain, 26 vols. (New Haven, CT: Yale University Press, 1957–2009), 18:110.

26. Jonathan Edwards, *Miscellanies*, no. 702, in *The Works of Jonathan Edwards*, 18:298.

27. Reeves, *Delighting in the Trinity*, 56.

the Father created the heavens and the earth for and through his Son, by the Holy Spirit. We say it, profess it, and sing it, ushered as we are into an ancient, heavenly hymn harmonized by God himself. God is a life-giving harmony of persons. If it were not so, God would not exist, nor would anything else. Whether theological or musical, harmonies are powerful. As Robert Jenson artfully notes, "God is a great *fugue*. There is nothing so capacious as a fugue."[28] Theology is most powerful when it sings.

Created in His Own Image

God exists because God is Trinity, and all of creation exists because God is the Trinity. And yet we can and must go one splendid step further: human beings exist because God is Trinity. The Trinity is not an addendum to our doctrine of God or our doctrine of creation, and the same holds true for our doctrine of humankind. If our anthropology does not require that God be Trinity or, for that matter, that God the Son be incarnate, then our understanding of humanity can hardly be called *Christ-ian*. Because God is triune, and humans are the *imago Dei*—the image *of God*—human existence is necessarily determined by God's fundamental nature. This makes the oft-repeated beginning to John Calvin's *Institutes of the Christian Religion* worth pondering anew: "Nearly all the wisdom we possess, that is to say, true and sound wisdom, consists of two parts: the knowledge of God and of ourselves."[29] As Calvin knew well, the order is crucial; true, godly wisdom demands the acknowledgment that human existence is not self-explanatory; it depends on our knowledge of God. Who we confess God to be defines who we confess humans to be.

This confession is all the more urgent in our day, in a culture where the definition of humanity seems to hang ever more in the balance.

28. Robert W. Jenson, *Systematic Theology*, vol. 1, *The Triune God* (New York: Oxford University Press, 1997), 236 (emphasis original).
29. John Calvin, *Inst.* 1.1.1.

Contemporary anthropological scales are increasingly tipped in favor of a legion of ideological forces that are actually misanthropic in nature, each seeking in its own way to weigh in on, and weigh down, the nature of human existence. The gravity and force of such anti-Christian ideologies cannot be underestimated, since they suffuse the political and cultural air that Christians breathe. Technophilia, individualism, sexual revolutionism, abortionism, racism, sexism, and ageism, to name but a few of the most prominent misanthropies, each imply and seek to support anthropologies lethally aligned against, and fundamentally at odds with, reality. In the context of such anthropological animus, the church must be all the more resolute in her confession that human beings are the image of God, who was, is, and ever shall be a holy communion of three-personal love. Apart from such a confession, the church will be tried and tempted by seducers aiming to replace God's image with their own. If we do not begin knowing ourselves by first knowing God in Christ, our self-knowledge will inevitably become self-referential, breeding a host of anthropological errors, each more confused and confusing than the last.

A truly Christian confession of the nature of the human person must thus be founded on christological and trinitarian grounds. James B. Torrance is right to insist,

> What is needed today is a better understanding of the person not just as an individual but as someone who finds his or her true being in communion with God and with others, the counterpart of a trinitarian doctrine of God. . . . God is love and has his true being in communion, in the mutual indwelling of Father, Son and Holy Spirit—*perichōrēsis*, the patristic word. This is the God who has created us male and female in his image to find our true humanity in perichoretic unity with him and one another, and who renews us in his image in Christ.[30]

---

30. James B. Torrance, *Worship, Community and the Triune God of Grace* (Downers Grove, IL: IVP Academic, 1996), 38.

All non-Christian and sub-Christian anthropologies have one thing in common: they do not have a "counterpart" to the Trinity. For example, individualism, which is to be carefully distinguished from individuality, is an anthropological heresy—not because it is "non-theistic" but because it is nontrinitarian and, thus, not finally Christian. Individual-*ism*, the conviction that persons can be defined in autonomous isolation from other persons, implies a doctrine of God that is altogether unlike God. Individualism is pregnant with a species of solipsism (self-reference) that gives birth to tragic anthropological absurdities such as technophilia, homoeroticism, transgenderism, racism, abortionism, and sexism. Each says something about God because each says something about how God is to be imaged in his human creatures. Christians are not opposed to such anthropological aberrations on primarily social, political, psychological, or moral grounds, as important as such may be. We oppose these distortions of authentic human existence because they are literally un-*godly*— they do not reflect or echo the reality of God. Anthropologies that require no more than a naked theism for their foundation—that do not require a God who is fecund and capacious, self-giving and life giving—are prone to distort the meaning and destiny of the human being. A lonely, solitary, sterile God may be sufficient to account for the creation of Adam, but a triune God is necessary to account for Eve and the fruit of her womb.

A generic theism is simply insufficient as a foundation for "knowledge of ourselves." Scott Swain is right: "The doctrine of the Trinity is not simply one article among many within the Christian confession. It is the first and fundamental article of the faith, and the framework within which all other articles receive their meaning and import, because the Triune God is the efficient, restorative, and perfecting principle of all things in nature, grace, and glory."[31] What obtains for all other articles certainly obtains for a Christian accounting of the

---

31. Scott R. Swain, "Divine Trinity," in *Christian Dogmatics: Reformed Theology for the Church Catholic*, ed. Michael Allen and Scott R. Swain (Grand Rapids: Baker Academic, 2016), 78.

human being. The meaning and import of anthropology ("knowledge of ourselves") must be framed within a realistic understanding of theology ("knowledge of God"). If the decisive fact of God's triune being has no constitutional bearing on our understanding of who we are, it becomes difficult to imagine how the doctrine of the Trinity truly touches on our understanding of reality. With great gladness, the church is able to rejoice and take assurance in the very good news that God has created human beings as a reflection of who he truly is. Just as God is a being whose existence is defined by his interpersonal relationality (he would not be God otherwise), so too he has created us in such a way that our existence is defined by our interpersonal relationality (we would not be humans otherwise). If God were not a communion of life-giving persons, he would not exist; if we were not a communion of life-giving persons, we would not exist. We are the image of God.[32]

God Loves Because God Is

"God is love" is a statement so apparently self-evident and obvious that it has been reduced to the level of a *truism*, the kind of truth that requires no explanation. Count C. S. Lewis among the skeptics: "All sorts of people are fond of repeating the Christian statement that 'God is love.' But they seem not to notice that the words 'God is love' have no real meaning unless God contains at least two Persons. Love is something that one person has for another person. If God was a single person, then before the world was made, He was not love."[33] It is more than a little interesting that Lewis refers to the statement "God is love" as a specifically "Christian statement," since nearly

32. John D. Zizioulas writes, "The only way for a true person to exist is for being and communion to coincide. The triune God offers in Himself the only possibility for such an identification of being with communion; He is the revelation of true personhood." *Being as Communion: Studies in Personhood and the Church* (Crestwood, NY: St. Vladimir's Seminary Press, 1985), 107.

33. C. S. Lewis, *Mere Christianity*, rev. and exp. ed. (New York: HarperOne, 2015), 174.

all peoples, of any and every religious type, happily state the same truth. The clear implication from Lewis is that, unless God is an interpersonal communion—indeed, a Trinity of persons—then God is not, and cannot be, love. Even if we were to imagine, speculatively and theoretically, that God is *able to* love others outside himself if he were not triune, that is very different from stating that God *is* love. The first is an assertion about what God happens to do, the other is a much more important affirmation about who God essentially is. Jesus mercifully stops us short of the temptation to generalize God's love—as if his love could be known, appropriated, or co-opted under some condition in which God is other than Father, Son, and Spirit. The very good news that God loves us is based on a prior reality that God is himself the love by which he loves. The love that we come to experience in knowing Christ is a very particular love; it is in fact nothing less and nothing other than the eternal love by which God the Father has eternally loved God the Son "before the foundation of the world" (John 17:24). The love that Jesus brings to the world in the power of the Spirit, we must stress, is exactly and specifically the love that he has eternally and indissolubly known in his Father. Confessing this, we are prepared to hear the startling words of prayer that extend from Jesus's lips to his Father's ears: "I made known to them your name, and I will continue to make it known, *that the love with which you have loved me may be in them*, and I in them" (John 17:26). In his self-giving, Jesus does not, indeed cannot, give the world any other love.

God's love is "original" in the most literal sense: it originates in him. Just such an affirmation is necessary to forestall the assumptions that God's love is predicated on what or whom he creates or is merely some sort of abstract, cosmic entity that exists independently of him. Both assumptions are tragically anthropocentric, since they seek to define the love of God, and love in general, as a concept or ideal accessible and understandable apart from God's inner being and self-revelation. The tragedy lies in the abstraction: seeking to define "love" apart from God's inner nature leaves us with only a "concept" of love, which tends to be plastic and ephemeral, free-floating and arbitrary. Apart from Jesus, we are no better positioned to distinguish God from Satan than we are love from hate. This is a point punctuated by millennia of malice, cruelty, and bloodshed carried out in the name of "God" and "love" (no less "justice" and "freedom," which too are but empty, amorphous ideologies when abstracted from Christ). Apart from Jesus, one person's love may be another's hatred, and vice versa.

We need look no further than Scripture for evidence of this confusion. For it was Jesus himself, the very embodiment of the eternal love of God almighty, who became the object of the world's hatred. The world hated him first (John 15:18). How could that be? What kind of tragic transposition of love and hate could render the ultimate and definitive expression of God's love the object of human hatred, save that the world had embraced a concept of love that had no need of *theo-logy*: the Word of God? If Jesus became the target of the world's hatred—crucify him!—then love must have been hanged on the cross: crucified, dead, and buried. On goes the tragic quest for an ideal unmoored from its foundation in the heart of God, in which humanity searches and scrapes after "love" in the wake of his death and burial. If love was put to death, then "love" would thereafter need to be defined apart from Jesus, apart from God; love was mortified, slain in God's name.

In one of the greatest paradoxes in human and divine history, the death of love occasioned its resurrection. The love of God, manifested in Christ Jesus, became the stimulant for human hatred, and yet human hatred was stayed and stifled in the name of divine love. The love of the Father for his beloved Son was the only love strong enough to resurrect love from its burial. And so Jesus crucified all concepts of love that take no account of him; and then raised love from the dead, securing it in the heart of his Father once again. In Jesus Christ, and only in him, love was returned to its place in the life of God, in the *koinonia* of the Spirit. And now, through the fellowship of the Spirit, we may know the very love of God, in the grace of the

Lord Jesus Christ (2 Cor. 13:14). Thomas F. Torrance captures this triune truth beautifully and powerfully:

> In the outgoing movement of his eternal Love God himself has come among us and become one of us and one with us in the Person of his beloved Son in order to reconcile us to himself and to share with us the Fellowship of Love which he has within his own Triune Life. . . . The Love that God the Father, God the Son and God the Holy Spirit eternally are, has taken incarnate form in the Lord Jesus Christ for us and our salvation.[34]

> The Gospel does not rest simply on the fact that God loves us, but on the fact that he loves us with the very same Love which he is in the eternal Communion of Love which God is in his Triune Being.[35]

Love, we are repeatedly told, "makes the world go 'round." How true! But there is no love that can revolutionize the world apart from the Trinity, and there is no world to "go 'round" that does not originate in the love of the Father for the Son in the Spirit. The only love capable of animating the world is a love able to overcome death. So, with due respect to the eloquent waxings of poets and philosophers, and to all well-intentioned imaginations and conceptions of love generated by a world that put love to death, the church takes refuge in a love that has *overcome* the world.

That is why, when the church says "love," she means the love of the Father, Son, and Holy Spirit. It is their three-personal love that created the world, that same love alone that re-created it, and the only love that can sustain it. The church exists in a world that has put love to death, but she exists no less in a world in which love has been raised again in the Lord Jesus. In Christ, the church knows love's death but also its resurrection. As John Donne knew so well, unless we are fettered by God's triune love, we cannot be free; unless

---

34. Torrance, *Christian Doctrine of God*, 162.
35. Torrance, *Christian Doctrine of God*, 253.

we are ravished, we cannot be chaste; and unless we are broken, we cannot be healed:

> Batter my heart, three-person'd God; for you
> As yet but knocke, breathe, shine, and seeke to mend;
> That I may rise, and stand, o'erthrow mee, and bend
> Your force, to breake, blowe, burn and make me new.
> I, like an usurpt towne, to another due,
> Labour to admit you, but Oh, to no end,
> Reason your viceroy in mee, mee should defend,
> But is captiv'd, and proves weake or untrue.
> Yet dearly I love you, and would be loved faine,
> But am betroth'd unto your enemie:
> Divorce mee, untie, or breake that knot againe,
> Take mee to you, imprison mee, for I
> Except you enthrall mee, never shall be free,
> Nor ever chast, except you ravish mee.[36]

Theology stands or falls in relation to this thrice-personal God. Unless the church's theology is a reflection of her encounter with the pure joy that comes from being dazzled and romanced by the love of God the Holy Trinity, that theology will never be free.

36. John Donne, "Holy Sonnet XIV," in *John Donne: A Selection of His Poetry*, ed. John Hayward (London: Penguin, 1950), 171–72.

The Body of Christ

The Ecclesial Context of Christian Theology

Fix your mind's eye on the majestic Mount Rushmore. But rather than picturing the faces of four American presidents, imagine it bedecked with four great Christian theologians. Who might they be? Athanasius, Teresa of Ávila, John Calvin, and Jonathan Edwards make a formidable foursome. Yet Hilary of Poitiers, Julian of Norwich, Martin Luther, and Charles Spurgeon are worthy candidates too. And we must not forget Ignatius and Irenaeus, Ambrose and Augustine, Macrina the Younger and Maximus the Confessor, Anselm and Aquinas, Thomas Cranmer and Hilda of Whitby, John Wesley and John Stott. Still, we have scarcely scratched the surface. Choosing so select a group from such an embarrassment of riches is beyond difficult; it is nearly impossible. Only a vast range of mountains could come close to containing the countenances of the most faithful and fruitful theologians to finish the race we now run. Were we to behold such a spectacle, many differences would emerge in our glorious company of companions. But among their far more numerous similarities, none shine brighter than this: they were each and all ablaze with unfeigned love for the church and fully immersed in her life and ministry.

Wholehearted immersion in the life and ministry of the church is a mark of *every* Christian who is earnest about answering Jesus's call to follow him, and this call invariably involves theological formation. For the blood and breath of true theology is the presence of God, known amid the people of God; true theologians are thus made within the church, to act for the church, in the name of the church.[1] Our Christian forebears knew well that the native and natural habitat for theological formation is the church, because theological formation is conformity to Christ, the ultimate theologian and the head of the church. Only in modernity are efforts made to move theology to the margins of the church and beyond, away from the convictions and practices of the Christian life.[2] Such efforts are injurious to the church and theology alike, since misplaced, misguided theology tempts the church to be fearful and suspicious of one of God's most precious gifts: the vocation of theology that is rightfully hers to cherish and steward. Meanwhile, the oxymoronic enterprise of nonecclesial theology delivers not the relational, dialogical knowledge of Christ gained in the church but, at best, secondhand divinity and the lonesome monologue of self-talk that characterizes all secular religion. Depending on the hearts and hands that further it, theology can be holy or unholy, sacred or diabolical—our conscience and compass or a coat of chain mail that crushes and freezes us.[3] It is imperative, therefore, that theology be done in a churchly context, where now as ever, true theologians are born and brought to maturity.

The Body of Christ

The Bible is a wellspring of rich ecclesial imagery, depicting the church as wife, bride, mother, city, flock, temple, vineyard, garden,

1. Helmut Thielicke, *A Little Exercise for Young Theologians*, trans. Charles L. Taylor (1962; repr., Grand Rapids: Eerdmans, 1998), 4–5; James B. Torrance, *Worship, Community and the Triune God of Grace* (Downers Grove, IL: IVP Academic, 1996), 10.

2. Ellen T. Charry, *By the Renewing of Your Minds: The Pastoral Function of Christian Doctrine* (New York: Oxford University Press, 1997), 5, 245.

3. Helmut Thielicke, *Out of the Depths*, trans. G. W. Bromiley (Grand Rapids: Eerdmans, 1962), 54–55; Thielicke, *A Little Exercise for Young Theologians*, 36–38.

chosen race, holy nation, family of God, and still more. Feminine imagery is plentiful, and with good reason. These images beautifully accentuate the archetypically feminine functions of the church, as believers are conceived in her womb, nourished at her bosom, and continually fortified by her care, comfort, and correction. Moreover, these feminine images highlight that the church's union with Jesus Christ is humanizing and personalizing, such that the church is not an inanimate and impersonal *it*, but a living and lavishly loved *she*. Just as surely as Jesus is the new Adam, the church is the new Eve (Rom. 5:12–21; 1 Cor. 15:20–23, 45–49). The first Adam and Eve were together the image of God as explicitly male and female in the creation of all things. Jesus and the church are the new Adam and Eve, together the restored image of God as explicitly male and female in the renewal of all things. God caused a deep sleep to fall on the first Adam and from his opened side fashioned the first Eve. And God caused the deeper sleep of death to fall on the new Adam and from his pierced side fashioned the new Eve. The first Eve is the mother of all the living, and the new Eve is the mother of all who are fully alive in Christ (Gen. 1:26–27; 2:18–23; 3:20; Eph. 5:22–33). Yes, the feminine predominates in this wellspring of imagery for the church. And all these images must be taken into account so that they may inform, modify, and qualify each other in providing a profound complex of meaning for us to behold the bride of Christ in her multifaceted splendor.[4]

Yet Scripture does not simply pour forth images for the church and leave us to contrive abstract, arbitrary connections among them. One image gathers up and holds together all others: *the body of Christ*. Here we have the most theological and theologically instructive image of all, because it refers us directly to Jesus Christ himself, the sole

---

4. Paul J. Griffiths, "Christians and the Church," in *The Oxford Handbook of Theological Ethics*, ed. Gilbert Meilaender and William Werpehowski (New York: Oxford University Press, 2005), 398; John C. Clark and Marcus Peter Johnson, *The Incarnation of God: The Mystery of the Gospel as the Foundation of Evangelical Theology* (Wheaton: Crossway, 2015), 214–24.

head and Savior of the church (Eph. 5:23). The term *body* is crucial, because it applies to both Christ and the church; and this body alerts us to the divine-humanity of the church, because this body is the body *of Christ*. We are thus precluded from falsely reducing the church to only her institutional, sociological, or anthropological facets—to some mere human entity that stands in place of the God-man or, worse, that stands between us and the God-man. For the church stands *with* the God-man, having her existence and identity in that most intimate of all one-flesh unions, in the one body that makes all believers living members of our incarnate Lord himself (1 Cor. 12:27; Col. 1:18, 24).[5]

Let us be clear: the church's existence and identity is not at all ethereal, ambiguous, or amorphous but a bodily reality as concrete as the embodied Christ. Simon Chan notes, "The expression *body of Christ* is more than a metaphor for some intimate social dynamic between Christ and his church. It is an ontological reality, as Christ is ontologically real."[6] So profound is this one-flesh union that when his church is persecuted, Jesus cries, "Why are you persecuting me?" (Acts 9:1–5). As the apostle Paul explains, "No one ever hated his own flesh, but nourishes and cherishes it, just as Christ does the church, because we are members of his body" (Eph. 5:29–30). In fact, Paul extols the nature of this relationship in even more jaw-dropping fashion, declaring that the church "is his [Christ's] body, the fullness of him who fills all in all" (Eph. 1:23).[7] To be sure, God the Son lacks nothing in himself and does all things out of divine plenitude, not deficit. Yet in the overflow of his goodness, he considers

5. Thomas F. Torrance, "What Is the Church?," *The Ecumenical Review* 11, no. 1 (October 1958): 6–7.

6. Simon Chan, *Liturgical Theology: The Church as Worshipping Community* (Downers Grove, IL: IVP Academic, 2006), 27 (emphasis original).

7. Paul's statement is arresting in English yet is even more emphatic in Greek: *hētis estin to sōma autou*—the church, "which is [indeed, or in truth] his body." See Harold W. Hoehner, *Ephesians: An Exegetical Commentary* (Grand Rapids: Baker Academic, 2002), 290; Frank Thielman, *Ephesians*, Baker Exegetical Commentary on the New Testament (Grand Rapids: Baker Academic, 2010), 112.

himself complete only when we are one with him. God deemed it "not good" when the first Adam was without the first Eve, so how unfathomably good it is that the new Adam is now and evermore in flesh-of-flesh, bone-of-bone bond with the new Eve (Gen. 2:18; Eph. 5:31–32). Jesus is the whole Christ—head and members—in the fullness of his union with the church, who is to abide in him as he abides in her (John 15:4–5). The church, in turn, exists and acts as church in the world by virtue of the enduring presence of Jesus, who promises, "I am with you always, to the end of the age" (Matt. 28:20). Joyfully, therefore, we sing, "There is one body and one Spirit[,] . . . one Lord, one faith, one baptism, one God and Father of all, who is over all and through all and in all" (Eph. 4:4–6).

Given the ontological reality of the relationship between Jesus Christ and his church, he is present with and in the church as the essence [Latin, *esse*] of the church. The Nicene Creed states this core Christian conviction with lucid brevity: "We believe . . . in one, holy, catholic, and apostolic Church."[8] The church is *one* because she is in Christ, just as Christ is in the Father, and the Father is in him (John 17:20–23); the church is *holy* because she is sanctified in Christ by the Spirit as the communion of saints (1 Cor. 1:2; 2 Cor. 1:1; Eph. 1:1; Phil. 1:1; Col. 1:2); the church is *catholic* because all the saints in all times and places are a universal whole in Christ, and thus individually members of one another (Rom. 12:5; 1 Cor. 12:12–13; Eph. 3:6); and the church is *apostolic* because she is the witness and fellowship of the apostles, and Christ never wills to be known without the apostles, and us in them (John 15:26–27; 1 John 1:1–4). Indeed, the one, holy, catholic, and apostolic church has life and being because the whole fullness of God's triune deity dwells bodily in Christ, and Christ's body is the church (Col. 1:18–19, 24; 2:9).

Only the presence of Christ can save, sustain, and perfect a people. And Christ is now and *evermore* incarnate. Therefore, just as surely as Christ is never without his body, he is never without his church,

8. "The Constantinopolitan Creed (381)," in CC, 33.

because his body includes—*incorporates*—his church.[9] John Calvin wisely warns Christians not to "contemplate him [Christ] outside ourselves from afar . . . because we put on Christ and are engrafted into his body—in short, because he deigns to make us one with him."[10] To contemplate Christ removed from his church is to entertain the macabre monstrosity of a dismembered Christ and a decapitated church, which at once disfigures our Lord, ourselves, and our fellow members of his body. In other words, the falsehood of a distant, inaccessible, virtual Christ reduces the church to a hollow, wraithlike travesty of her true self. And in such a state she can be perceived as little more than an odd amalgam of historical society, social club, and charitable agency, a voluntary gathering of like-minded people trying to preserve the memory and teachings of Jesus, promote mutual support, and provide religious goods and services to advance public interests and agendas. But the church is far more than that!

Clearly, the biblical reality of *body* is foundational to our theological formation, not least because any truly *Christ-ian* theology of bodies must be calibrated by that most important of all bodies: the human body of the Second Person of the Trinity. Our bodies, and the body of the church, are rightly understood in terms of his body. For Christ's own body is the criterion for distinguishing real from fanciful notions of these bodies, since all that is real about these bodies derives from and depends on the reality of his. So we must understand that Christ's body is both individual and communal, the body of one person intimately and essentially related to other persons, divine and human. No mutual exclusion exists between individuality and community. In fact, our Lord's individuality is *rooted* in community, such that his particular personhood is recognized precisely as he participates bodily in the life of God and humanity. Indeed, Christ's body is that of God the Son and the Son of Mary, God with us as one of us, the true and full image of God as true and full man: the

9. Christopher R. J. Holmes, "The Church and the Presence of Christ: Defending Actualist Ecclesiology," *Pro Ecclesia* 21, no. 3 (July 2012): 268–69.

10. John Calvin, *Inst.* 3.11.10.

God-man. He has come in the name of the Father to do only and all the Father's will, granting the church to participate in his body, given for the life of the world (John 5:30–31, 43; 6:51; 1 Cor. 10:14–17). There is thus one truly authentic existence and aim for our bodies. In the body of the church, in life-giving, life-transforming communion with the embodied Christ, "we are to grow up in every way into him who is the head, into Christ, from whom the whole body, joined and held together by every joint with which it is equipped, when each part is working properly, makes the body grow so that it builds itself up in love" (Eph. 4:15–16).[11]

Christ's own body bears witness that authentic embodiment is individual and communal, that real individuality is situated, exercised, and discerned in real community. Consequently, that most real of all bodies demythologizes the ideologies of individualism and collectivism, showing them to be fanciful, distorted notions of embodiment. For individualism falsely invests us with autonomy and self-sufficiency, grounding one's identity in the name and will of the independent, solitary self; thus individualism destroys real community by denaturing real individuality, in the end forfeiting both. Yet collectivism falsely divests us of actual place and value, grounding the self in tribalized sociopolitical structures, such that the personal and particular is eclipsed by the name and will of identitarian groups or movements; thus collectivism destroys real individuality by denaturing real community, in the end forfeiting both. The individual and communal aspects of authentic embodiment stand or fall together, because Christ is their true ground. So despite their differences, individualism and collectivism are similar in the most momentous ways. Both are ultimately groundless, since both contradict the reality of Christ's body and thus what is real about our bodies and the body of the church. Individual human bodies are made to image Christ as living members of the community of an individual church body. Likewise, individual church bodies are made to image Christ as particular

11. Griffiths, "Christians and the Church," 400–401.

expressions of the communal body that extends through time and across space—the universal church, or church catholic. No individual person or church can truly image Christ as an independent person or church, because independent persons must spurn the God with whom Christ is one, just as independent churches must spurn the bride with whom Christ is one. And no tribalized, identitarian group or movement can supplant that unique community of which Christ is the sole head and singular Savior.

The fact of the matter is that the native and natural habitat for truly *Christ-ian* theological formation always has been, and ever shall be, the church. Jesus Christ is more than the substance and sum of theology. He is the ultimate theologian, the living God-Word who speaks and acts, giving definite place, shape, and content to theology through his presence in the church. This is at once a heavenly presence and an earthly presence, a spiritual presence and a bodily presence. For the same Son who assumed and exalted humanity to heavenly existence with the Father by the power of the Spirit has earthly existence in one-flesh union with the church; and the church is nothing less or other than the fullness of Christ's body (Eph. 1:22–23). Surely Christ does not exist *as* the church—the church is not absorbed in Christ, an extension of Christ, or interchangeable with Christ. But just as surely, the church is no proxy for Christ, in which case the church could not live and thrive in the effulgent beauty of Christ's presence but only wither and die in the vacuous horror of his absence. Instead, Christ's relationship with the church is one of distinction without separation or division. He makes the church his own while ever remaining the church's head and Lord, like he made human nature his own while ever remaining his divine self in relation to us. What is true of the church is thus true of her members. God the Son became human not so we may become God but so we may become one with God—so we may become our true selves, and the church her true self, in union with Christ's self.[12]

---

12. Holmes, "The Church and the Presence of Christ," 271–74.

"Come, follow me!" When Jesus Christ issues this call, it is lavish invitation and lordly command—laden with promise (Matt. 4:19; 16:24; 19:28; Mark 1:17; 10:21; Luke 5:27; 18:22; John 1:43; 8:12; 21:19). So let us hear and heed it for what it truly is: our sacred summons to the *person* of Christ, and to the *place* of Christ. For Jesus calls us to himself, and to the church that is his body. He calls us to a life of faith and obedience that unveils our eternal destiny, and to the locale where he gives himself to us in word and sacrament infused with the power of the Spirit.[13] This call is issued repeatedly and answered in kind, giving cadence and antiphonal texture to our lifelong journey of discipleship. In fact, the call-and-answer dialogue that marks this journey is enacted weekly in the worship of Great Tradition churches: Christians leave their hearths and homes, their gardens and garages, their places of work and stations of life in the world, to come to the church. The journey begins with the processional, when, following Jesus, depicted by the processional cross, the gathered people of God are led by their Lord into the triune presence of God. Accenting the journey's advent, they then declare, "Blessed be God: Father, Son, and Holy Spirit. And blessed be his kingdom, now and for ever. Amen."[14] Amen indeed! The person of Christ meets us in the place of Christ, leading the body of which he is head to the heart of human existence, history, and creation. Alexander Schmemann explains:

> From the beginning the destination is announced: the journey is to the Kingdom. This is where we are going—and not symbolically, but really. In the language of the Bible, which is *the* language of the Church, to bless the Kingdom is not simply to acclaim it. It is to declare it to be the goal, the end of all our desires and interests, of our whole life, the supreme and ultimate value of all that exists. To bless is to accept in love, and to move toward what is loved and accepted. The Church

13. Dietrich Bonhoeffer, *Christ the Center*, trans. Edwin H. Robertson (New York: Harper & Row, 1978), 59–60; Keith L. Johnson, *Theology as Discipleship* (Downers Grove, IL: IVP Academic, 2015), 37.

14. *The Book of Common Prayer* (New York: Oxford University Press, 1979), 323.

thus is the assembly, the gathering of those to whom the ultimate destination of all life has been revealed and who have accepted it. This acceptance is expressed in the solemn . . . Amen. It is indeed one of the most important words in the world, for it expresses the agreement of the Church to follow Christ in His ascension to His Father, to make this ascension the destiny of man. It is Christ's gift to us, for only in Him can we say Amen to God, or rather He himself is our Amen to God and the Church is an Amen to Christ. Upon this Amen the fate of the human race is decided. It reveals that the movement toward God has begun.[15]

Because Christ is the substance and sum of theology, theological formation is conformity to Christ. And because Christ is the ultimate theologian, the primary and principal context for theological formation is the body he nourishes and cherishes as his own. Therefore, if "Amen" voices the church's agreement to follow Christ, it affirms that theological formation is elemental to answering Christ's call, an essential for the journey that includes the entire church, excluding or exempting none. The news is sweet, since the call is sublime: "Come to me, all who labor and are heavy laden, and I will give you rest. Take my yoke upon you, and learn from me, for I am gentle and lowly in heart, and you will find rest for your souls" (Matt. 11:28–29). Come to me. Take my yoke. Learn from me. Theological formation is not the stuff of secondhand, historical knowledge *about* Christ, the sort we might gain about Cleopatra or Charlemagne in lecture halls, libraries, and museums. Reading, studying, and the like are crucial to holistic Christian maturity and must never be diminished or despised. But there is no substitute for the firsthand, relational, dialogical knowledge *of* Christ learned in the church as Christ joins his life to ours, as we "share in a heavenly calling" together with Christ (Heb. 3:1).[16] Given the tutelage had only in Christ's keep and care, Martin Luther

---

15. Alexander Schmemann, *For the Life of the World: Sacraments and Orthodoxy*, 2nd ed. (Crestwood, NY: St. Vladimir's Seminary Press, 2002), 29 (emphasis original).

16. Johnson, *Theology as Discipleship*, 74.

vows that "experience alone makes the theologian."[17] And Thomas Torrance speaks of the yoke that is the church's participation in Christ:

> Through union with Jesus Christ the church shares in his life and in all that he has done for mankind. Through his birth its members have a new birth and are made members of the new humanity. Through his obedient life and death their sins are forgiven and they are clothed with a new righteousness. Through his resurrection and triumph over the powers of darkness they are freed from the dominion of evil and are made one body with him. Through his ascension the kingdom of heaven is opened to all believers and the church waits for his coming again to fulfill in all humanity the new creation which he has already begun in it. Thus the church finds its life and being not in itself but in Jesus Christ alone, for not only is he the head of the church but he includes the church within his own fullness.[18]

Seeking Life in the Self: On Fanciful Theologies

Gnosticism emerged in the first century as an eclectic collection of sects and doctrines, posing an enormous and enduring challenge to the church. Early Gnostics looked askance at the fidelity of ordinary Christians to orthodox teaching and practice, offering instead an enlightened, privatized knowledge (Greek, *gnōsis*) reserved for superior souls, spiritual elites. This so-called knowledge incited debauchery for some and body-despising asceticism for others. But the basic conviction of early Gnostics was the stark opposition of the spiritual and the material, meaning that things physical and bodily were considered contrary to the divine and inferior to one's interior self. The heresy of Gnosticism has proven resilient, living and thriving among us today.[19]

---

17. Martin Luther, "Table Talk Recorded by Veit Dietrich," in *LW*, 54:7.

18. Thomas F. Torrance, *Atonement: The Person and Work of Christ*, ed. Robert T. Walker (Downers Grove, IL: IVP Academic, 2009), 361.

19. Hans Urs von Balthasar, introduction to *The Scandal of the Incarnation: Irenaeus "Against the Heresies,"* by Irenaeus, trans. John Saward (San Francisco: Ignatius, 1990), 1–4.

Neo-Gnostics are more earthbound than their forebears, yet family traits are telling. For while ancient Gnostics tried to escape the world of matter for a purely spiritual existence, modern Gnostics try to escape the world of the mundane for a purely pleasurable existence. While ancient Gnostics tried to escape their physical bodies to become perfected spiritual beings, modern Gnostics try to escape their real bodies to become perfected bodies, like the computer-generated, Photoshopped, and often ambiguously gendered bodies routinely paraded before us. And while ancient Gnostics embraced an anti-material essentialism to seek the true god within, modern Gnostics embrace a psychological or therapeutic essentialism to seek their true self within. Gnosticism old and new is thus about vague, malleable "spirituality" in service of self-invention, about fleeing anything from without that may critique, contradict, or lay lordly claim on things within.[20]

Modern naturalism also insists on the stark opposition of the spiritual and the material. But naturalism holds materialism as its basic conviction, an anti-spiritual essentialism that denies the existence of anything that cannot be reduced to an exclusively physical composition. As such, the world is seen as self-existing, not divinely created and sustained. Humanity is the product of totally natural processes, not fearfully and wonderfully made in the divine image. All things are contained in a closed cosmos, open to nothing beyond itself. Even the internal intricacies of our thought, affect, and will are but bodily effects of prior physical causes. Materialists are atheists, seeing humans as at last come of age, subject to no other lords than themselves, save the laws of nature. Yet the anti-spiritual essentialism that naturalists share does not mean naturalists are anti-religion. In fact, according to the famed *A Humanist Manifesto*, modern naturalism is itself a religion—a *godless* religion with the self-appointed agenda of offering "a new statement of the means and purposes of religion." This document then announces that naturalism finds "the

---

20. Mark Sayers, *Disappearing Church: From Cultural Relevance to Gospel Resilience* (Chicago: Moody, 2016), 59–65.

complete realization of human personality to be the end of man's life and seeks its development and fulfillment in the here and now. . . . Though we consider the religious forms and ideas of our fathers no longer adequate, the quest for the good life is still the central task for mankind."[21]

Modern Gnosticism and naturalism are vastly different in their views of the spiritual and the material. Nonetheless, both exhibit what Charles Taylor calls the main feature of our secular age: the eclipse of goals and claims that transcend self-styled notions of human flourishing.[22] More to the point, both exemplify what David Bentley Hart calls the only religion that truly thrives in modernity: the "narrow service of the self, of the impulses of the will, of the nothingness that is all the withdrawal of Christianity leaves behind."[23] In other words, the secular age in which we live is neither nonreligious nor religiously neutral. The secular age is post-Christian, marked by widespread effort among social elites and market influencers to move culture beyond the impress of the Christian faith. So the present principalities and powers, the predominant and prevailing spirit of this age, is such that even religions so otherwise at odds as Gnosticism and materialism are both enthralled by the same set of vortex-like sentiments: one's ultimate authority is oneself; institutions and external authorities should be distrusted, yet personal inclinations and aspirations should not; the highest good is individual freedom and happiness, enabled by self-definition and self-expression; traditions, generational wisdom, and time-tested social structures that impede the pursuit of this highest good must be deconstructed and reshaped or destroyed and discarded; and the world improves with the advance

---

21. "Humanist Manifesto I (1933)," American Humanist Association, accessed November 12, 2020, https://www.americanhumanist.org/what-is-humanism/manifesto1/. See also Steve Wilkens and Mark L. Sanford, *Hidden Worldviews: Eight Cultural Stories That Shape Our Lives* (Downers Grove, IL: IVP Academic, 2009), 100–105.

22. Charles Taylor, *A Secular Age* (Cambridge, MA: Belknap, 2007), 19–21.

23. David Bentley Hart, *In the Aftermath: Provocations and Laments* (Grand Rapids: Eerdmans, 2009), 15.

of individual autonomy, such that, in the end, the cardinal social virtue is tolerance, the lack of which is intolerable.[24]

Theological Formation in the School of Christ

Christians are not called to long for former days when the Christian religion thrived nor future days when the Christian religion can compete with secular religion. For the Christian faith is not a species in the genus of religion. As Schmemann urges, Christianity "is in a profound sense the *end of all religion*. . . . Religion is needed where there is a wall of separation between God and man. But Christ who is both God and man has broken down the wall between man and God. He has inaugurated a new life, not a new religion."[25] The Christian faith is about the divine Word being fully human and about our bodies being conformed to his body. It is about the reconciliation of heaven and earth being shown as spiritual realities that are made known physically and materially in the body of the church. Therefore, Gnosticism and naturalism are not progressive but regressive, not on the right side of history but flat wrong about reality. Spirit and matter are not contradictory; they are complementary, which means neither may be despised or totalized. *Matter matters*—precisely because the Creator and Redeemer of matter is revealed and received through matter. Jesus Christ reveals the meaning of matter, the reality of the cosmos, as he unites in his body God and humanity, heaven and earth, spiritual and material—indeed, as he reveals himself to be the visible image of the invisible God (Col. 1:15). Every gift we receive from God we receive through Christ, the one mediator and only fount of all God's blessings. Leonard Vander Zee thus notes that "Christ is the quintessential sacrament, the visible sign of the invisible grace of God."[26] And Christ is the visible grace of God

---

24. Sayers, *Disappearing Church*, 15–17.
25. Schmemann, *For the Life of the World*, 19–20 (emphasis original).
26. Leonard J. Vander Zee, *Christ, Baptism and the Lord's Supper: Recovering the Sacraments for Evangelical Worship* (Downers Grove, IL: InterVarsity, 2004), 51.

not in vague, amorphous ways but in physical, material ways, not in opposition to or abstraction from the church but with and in the church. So as Christ is the sacrament of God, the church is the sacrament of Christ—the visible sign, the embodied locale, of our Lord's gracious presence and action.

Christians are thus called to loving and holy defiance of the spirit of this post-Christian age and its secular religion. This means devotion to the life of the church, pursuing theological formation in the school of Christ under the present and active headship of the Lord and *Logos* of theology himself. The curriculum is not privatized theology for an elite few but public theology for the entire body. Therefore, theological formation in the school of Christ requires a degree and depth of loyalty reserved for real—not fanciful—notions of bodies, rooted in that most real of all bodies, Christ's own. First, this loyalty requires us to cherish the church as the ever-living body of Christ and thus the tradition of the church as the living witness of the dead to Christ's abiding presence in the church through time. To deconstruct or discard this tradition is a capitulation to the spirit of this age that fails to honor thy fathers and mothers in the faith, much less the Christ who cherishes the church as his own flesh, blemishes and all. Loss of memory is loss of identity; and loss of identity is loss of catholicity.[27] Second, this loyalty requires us to cherish the church as the native and natural habitat, the primary and principal theater, of our theological formation. For theological formation happens first and foremost by embodied habituation in the church, as the church is that communal body in which our individual bodies are sanctified—habituated to holiness—by engaging in the acts of worship proper to Christ's body.[28] Theological formation definitely entails *in*formation, yet it is even more about *re*formation and *trans*formation by our participation in Christ according to the church's unique pattern of partnership with him. We learn by practice in the school of Christ

27. Chan, *Liturgical Theology*, 30–31.
28. Griffiths, "Christians and the Church," 403–4.

that these acts of worship are not just things *we* do; they are things through which something glorious is done *to* us.[29] Of this, then, we can be certain: it is not Christ who needs the present church but the church who needs Christ present. He is our living, active, and ultimate theologian in residence.

Listening and Hearing

Jesus Christ is the consummate listener, hearing the words of the Father *for us* in order to be the Word from the Father *to us* (John 5:30; 12:49; 14:31). As the Word, the very self-expression of God, Jesus proclaims, "My sheep hear my voice, . . . and they follow me" (John 10:27). Following is an act of faith, and faith comes from hearing. Yet Jesus's call does not pierce a placid silence. Rather, it joins a swirling din of competing calls and callers. The sheep follow Jesus not because his is the only voice; they follow him because they have come to know his voice, because they have learned to hear his voice by the practice of listening (John 10:3–5). Scripture tells of Jesus calling his sheep and then sending them to testify of him, fortified with this promise: "The one who hears you hears me, and the one who rejects you rejects me, and the one who rejects me rejects him who sent me" (Luke 10:16). To hear the disciples sent by Jesus is to hear Jesus and thus to share in Jesus's hearing of the Father. This sending of disciples culminates in the Gospels with the Great Commission, when Jesus declares, "All authority in heaven and on earth has been given to me. Go therefore and make disciples of all nations, . . . teaching them to observe all that I have commanded you. And behold, I am with you always, to the end of the age" (Matt. 28:18–20).

Because we are chronologically and geographically removed from events in the Gospels, we must ask: Is Jesus the Word from the Father who personally speaks to us still, or has he since fallen silent? May we also hear his voice, or is that gift reserved only for disciples of

---

29. James K. A. Smith, *You Are What You Love: The Spiritual Power of Habit* (Grand Rapids: Brazos, 2016), 19–22.

old? Is the Great *Commission* the church's sharing in Jesus's mission to the world, sealed by his promise to remain with us always, or his Great *Delegation* to a church he cheers remotely? Is theological formation about participation in the present and active Christ, or is it mere retrospection on a distant and dormant Christ? Augustine answers, "But perhaps someone thinks that, as He Himself came not to us, but sent, we have not heard His own voice, but only the voice of those whom He sent. Far from it: let such a thought be banished from your hearts; for He Himself was in those whom He sent. . . . It is He Himself who speaks by His servants, and it is His voice that is heard in those whom He sends."[30] The eternal Word incarnate and crucified, risen and exalted to the right hand of the Father, is resident and eloquent in his church. His exaltation does not entail isolation from the realm where he acted so mightily in the days of his humiliation. Rather, his exaltation is the condition of his continued address to the church, and this address takes the form of Scripture. By the action of the Spirit, the action of biblical writers is drawn into the action of Christ, so that these holy texts are truth of the Truth, words of the Word, making Scripture the precious vehicle of our ongoing encounter and acquaintance with the risen Lord. Theological formation depends on our hearing Scripture as the voice of the Good Shepherd, the Spirit-vivified herald of Jesus Christ's presence with his sheep in the here and now. Whenever Scripture speaks, Christ speaks—*and not just as the object of Scripture but as its living, acting subject.*[31]

Note the apostle Paul's commendation to the church in Thessalonica: "When you received the word of God, which you heard from us, you accepted it not as the word of men but as what it really is, the word of God, which is at work in you believers" (1 Thess. 2:13). At work indeed! Scripture again testifies: "For the word of God is living and active, sharper than any two-edged sword, piercing to the division of soul and of spirit, of joints and of marrow, and discerning

---

30. Augustine, *Tractates on the Gospel of John* 47.5, in NPNF[1], 7:262.
31. John Webster, *The Domain of the Word: Scripture and Theological Reason* (London: T&T Clark, 2012), 8, 32.

the thoughts and intentions of the heart. And no creature is hidden from *his* sight, but all are naked and exposed to the eyes of *him* to whom we must give account" (Heb. 4:12–13). The Word of God plumbs our depths—those rough and recalcitrant, shadowy and slippery places in our hearts that even the most insightful and intrepid self-analysis cannot reach. And the personal pronouns *his* and *him* highlight that we are searched and sorted out by that living and active Word who is the living and acting Christ. Scripture is thus to be prized as even more than the factually true and faithfully preserved record of when God *has* spoken in the past. Clearly, the initial location of Scripture is in history; but if this were Scripture's ultimate, determinative location, it would come to us lovely yet lifeless, like a butterfly pinned to a corkboard. Perhaps at that point we might resign ourselves to simply imitate examples and extract principles from Scripture. Perhaps we might subtly confuse Scripture for Christ as the one mediator between God and men (1 Tim. 2:5), unaware that even the noblest effort to infer or deduce Christ *from* Scripture is to deny that Christ speaks *in* Scripture. Whatever the case, Scripture would be viewed as little more than an ancient artifact.[32] This would result in our tragic failure to recognize that whenever Scripture is used to strengthen the saints, "the Father will send the promised Spirit, and the Son will loom before us to seize, save and sustain. Therefore Scripture never fails with respect to its purpose, an ever-renewed encounter with Jesus Christ."[33]

God is known in Christ, and Christ is known in Spirit-illumined knowledge of Scripture. This is the logic—the *Logos*, in fact—that forms and funds the manifold use of Scripture in the ministry of the church, seen most readily in preaching. Scripture assures us that we "have been born again, not of perishable seed but of imperishable, through the living and abiding word of God. . . . And this word is the good news that was preached to you" (1 Pet. 1:23, 25). The faithful

---

32. Webster, *Domain of the Word*, 20, 42.
33. Victor Shepherd, *Our Evangelical Faith* (Toronto: Clements, 2006), 29.

reading, teaching, and preaching of Scripture are thus anything but impotent acts of recitation and reflection. The Second Helvetic Confession, among the choicest fruits of the Reformation, states that the preached Word of God *is* the Word of God, in that Jesus Christ makes himself truly present to us in preaching: "Wherefore when this Word of God is now preached in the church by preachers lawfully called, we believe that the very Word of God is preached, and received of the faithful."[34] Luther muses, "I preach the gospel of Christ, and with my bodily voice I bring Christ into your heart, so that you may form him within yourself. . . . How much the poor bodily voice is able to do. First of all it brings the whole Christ to the ears; then it brings him into the hearts of all who listen and believe."[35] Mystery and miracle, Christ the divine *Logos* enters and possesses the human *logos*, visiting inestimable treasure upon earthen vessels to show that the surpassing power to bring light out of darkness belongs to God, not to us (2 Cor. 4:1–10). Bonhoeffer expands:

> The sermon is both the riches and the poverty of the Church. It is the form of the present Christ to which we are bound and to which we must hold. If the complete Christ is not in the preaching, then the Church is broken. The relation between God's Word and man's word in preaching is not that of mutual exclusion. The human word of preaching is not a phantom of the Word of God. Rather, God's Word has really entered into the humiliation of the words of men. Man's sermon is the Word of God, because God has freely bound himself and is bound to the words of men. . . . One cannot point to this word of man without pointing to this man Jesus who is God.[36]

Theological formation in the school of Christ teaches us not to divide or dichotomize the voice of the church from the voice of Christ, nor to confuse or conflate them. Indeed, the church speaks the truth

---

34. "The Second Helvetic Confession (1566)," in CC, 133.
35. Luther, "The Sacrament of the Body and Blood of Christ—Against the Fanatics," in *LW*, 36:340–41.
36. Bonhoeffer, *Christ the Center*, 52.

of Christ and does so authoritatively, yet only and ever as the church speaks the truth of Scripture, by which Christ exercises the lordly authority that is his alone in heaven and on earth. By practicing the act of listening to Scripture, we learn the art of hearing Scripture—the end of which is fellowship with the risen Christ. We learn to attend not chiefly to pastors and teachers, or even to prophets and apostles, but to the singular voice of our Good Shepherd, who addresses us no less truly and intimately than he did his disciples in the Upper Room or Mary Magdalene at the tomb on the morning of his resurrection. Following Christ means hearing and heeding Scripture, even and especially our Good Shepherd's hardest words in the most harrowing situations. For above all, it is in our own wildernesses, and our own Gethsemanes, that we learn to bear the pattern of partnership with him, that we come to know and rejoice in the reality that we live not by bread alone but by every word that comes from the mouth of God (Matt. 4:1–11; Luke 4:1–13). We practice the holy habit of testing voices—past and present, internal and external, of friends and foes, church and culture, and all others beside—by that one voice we must trust and obey in life and death. And our Lord performs the severe mercy of breaking down and building up, of plucking, planting, and pruning, from one degree of glory to another, conforming and transforming the whole of us to the whole of him (2 Cor. 3:18). So Augustine bids, "Let us consider at this time who we are, and ponder whom we hear. Christ is God, and He is speaking with men. He would have them to apprehend Him, let Him make them capable; He would have them to see Him, let Him open their eyes."[37]

Washing and Dining

Augustine notes the crucial connection between hearing and seeing in the school of Christ, and Calvin echoes this, stating that to mute the church's proclamation of Scripture "is like blotting out the face

---

37. Augustine, *Tractates on the Gospel of John*, 22.2, in NPNF[1], 7:145.

of God."[38] The chief teacher who presides in and over the church is none other than Christ, our ultimate theologian and Good Shepherd. Knowing and loving his voice frees us from idols and unholy strongholds, teaching us to think, speak, and act in accord with reality as our minds are renewed by the mind of Christ (Rom. 12:2; 1 Cor. 2:12–16; 2 Cor. 10:5). Still, our theological formation involves not only hearing the realities of the gospel but also seeing, even touching and tasting, the realities of the gospel. Conformity to the embodied Word in the body of the church calls for our whole-bodied engagement with Scripture and sacrament. For as the embodied Word is the visible sign of the invisible grace of God, the body of the church is the visible sign of his gracious presence and action. To his beloved church alone, therefore, Jesus Christ has personally mandated the two great sacraments of the gospel: baptism and the Eucharist (Matt. 28:19; Luke 22:19). Gifts of God for the people of God, these visible, tangible signs indelibly mark who the church is as the body of Christ and what Christ is accomplishing in her very midst.

Christ our theology, Christ the theologian, is the God-Word with us. Through baptism and the Eucharist he teaches us that the church's proclamation of the Word is to be both heard and seen, that the realities of the gospel are learned in the school of Christ by being washed in and dined on. For Scripture and the sacraments are complementary means to the same end: Jesus Christ, who is at once both Word of God and image of God. Scripture informs the sacraments with the gospel promises of Christ; and the sacraments, while adding no new content to the promises they attend, palpably clarify and confirm these promises. Just like Scripture, affirms Calvin, "Christ is the matter or (if you prefer) the substance of all the sacraments; for in him they have all their firmness, and they do not promise anything apart from him."[39] If it were the case that we receive *more* than Christ in the sacraments, their end would be beyond Christ himself. And if it were

---

38. Calvin, *Inst.* 4.1.5.
39. Calvin, *Inst.* 4.14.16.

the case that we receive *less* than Christ in the sacraments, they would signal not the real presence of Christ but the true absence of reality, reducing baptism and the Eucharist to quasi-Gnostic practices of pondering an inaccessible Savior. In either case, the sacraments would not complement, clarify, and confirm the gospel promises of Scripture but contradict and confuse them. What is actually the case is that together the audible words of Scripture and the tactile words of the sacraments grant us Spirit-enabled access to the incarnate Word—the life-giving, life-transforming presence of our Lord himself. "Therefore," says Calvin, "let it be regarded as a settled principle that the sacraments have the same office as the Word of God: to offer and set forth Christ to us, and in him the treasures of heavenly grace."[40]

Like Scripture, the sacraments do not set forth Christ without the ongoing action of God, as if they were inert and empty, simply prompts for us to publicly pledge our faithfulness and memorialize our redemption in Christ. Rather, the sacraments are primarily about God's action, about pointing and binding us to Christ and to one another as members of Christ's body. The relation between the Word of God *written* and the Word of God *incarnate* is one of distinction without separation, such that unholy violence is visited upon both by any attempt to conflate and confuse or divide and divorce them. And our Lord's relation to the audible words of Scripture is much like his relation to the tangible words of baptism and the Eucharist. When informed by the gospel and infused with the Spirit, the material—even mundane—elements of water, bread, and wine serve to deepen and strengthen our union with Christ, the *incorporation* of our bodies into his body and into the body of the church. On their journey to Canaan, the offspring of Abraham were delivered once and for all from bondage in Egypt through baptism into cloud and sea, then repeatedly fortified with spiritual food and drink "from the spiritual Rock" until their arrival in the promised land. Paul assures us that "the Rock was [the pre-incarnate] Christ" (1 Cor. 10:1–4).

40. Calvin, *Inst.* 4.14.17.

Similarly, on the church's journey to the kingdom, we are delivered once and for all from the bondage of sin and death through baptism into the incarnate Christ, then repeatedly nourished with his body and blood until at last we are safely home.

The term *baptism* is a transliteration of the Greek *baptisma*, which means immersion. Jesus's entering the River Jordan to receive baptism marks the beginning of his public ministry (Matt. 3:13–17; Mark 1:9–11; Luke 3:21–22; John 1:29–34). And Jesus explicitly ties his baptism at the Jordan to his crucifixion at Golgotha, calling the latter his baptism as well (Mark 10:38; Luke 12:50). Jordan and Golgotha loom at the opposite ends of Jesus's public ministry as two aspects of one comprehensive baptism, two facets of one fulfillment of all righteousness within the realm of our unrighteousness (Matt. 3:15; John 19:28–30). Jesus's baptism at the Jordan is the sign and seal of his immersion into the reality of identification with sin and sinners, of his entry into the state of human existence east of Eden to assume what is ours and make it his own (Matt. 3:6, 11; Mark 1:4; Acts 13:24; 19:4). And Jesus's baptism at Golgotha is the sign and seal of his immersion into the reality of divine judgment, of his bringing to completion God's condemnation of sin in the flesh he assumed for us and our salvation (Rom. 8:3; 2 Cor. 5:21). What, then, is our baptism? Immersion into Christ! For our baptism signs and seals the reality of our incorporation into the Savior crucified and resurrected for us, the truth of our participation in the baptismal identity of him who offered his complete and perfect filial righteousness to the Father as ours.[41] Once again, the Nicene Creed heralds this core Christian conviction: "We confess one baptism for the remission of sins."[42] That one baptism is Christ's, whose baptism provides context and efficacy—the pattern and power—for our baptism into him. Just as there is one Lord, one cross, one empty tomb, and one body, there is one baptism: the blessed baptism of our Lord,

---

41. Christian D. Kettler, *The Vicarious Humanity of Christ and the Reality of Salvation* (Eugene, OR: Wipf & Stock, 2010), 146–47.

42. "The Constantinopolitan Creed (381)," in CC, 33.

into whose broken and risen body the church and her members are immersed (Eph. 4:4–6).[43]

Hear the words of Scripture, the very Word of God: "Do you not know that all of us who have been baptized into Christ Jesus were baptized into his death? We were buried therefore with him by baptism into death, in order that, just as Christ was raised from the dead by the glory of the Father, we too might walk in newness of life" (Rom. 6:3–4; cf. Col. 2:11–12). Christ makes present in Scripture his voice and in baptism the unfading splendor and strength of his dying and rising. Therefore, the baptismal font does not adorn the school of Christ as a monument, where we merely pledge faith for exploits past, honoring him who died so we need not. The font is our tomb, where Christ bids us to come and die with him, so that we too may rise and live with him. Baptism is a bastion and bulwark of our theological formation, as the font neither topples nor totters before the lies, fads, and myths of this or any age. And because baptism is our immersion into Christ, it is our initiation into a theological formation that is part and parcel of our baptismal identity. Here our Lord teaches us that socially constructed, self-appointed identities are vapid and vain; that life is not an entitlement or an achievement but a gift dearly bought yet freely given; and that real meaning, freedom, and joy come not through self-justification and self-improvement, through moral grandstanding and virtue signaling, but through death with Christ to the flesh and the world (2 Cor. 5:16–17; Gal. 2:20; 6:14).[44]

---

43. Thomas F. Torrance, *Theology in Reconciliation: Essays towards Evangelical and Catholic Unity in East and West* (Eugene, OR: Wipf & Stock, 1996), 82–88.

44. It is precisely here, in light of the baptismal font, that the living Word of God declares: "For as many of you as were baptized into Christ have put on Christ. There is neither Jew nor Greek, there is neither slave nor free, there is no male and female, for you are all one in Christ Jesus" (Gal. 3:27–28; cf. Col. 3:9–11). Scripture readily affirms the reality of our ethnicity, sex, and stations in life yet utterly denies that these can constitute anything like an authentic identity. Baptism entails putting off and putting on, repudiating and receiving, and thus counting as rubbish even the world's most prized and praised identity markers in order that we may embrace and adore our baptismal identity, our communally grounded individuality as members of

Baptism is the sign and seal that our bodies are immersed at once into Christ's body and the body of the church. Our bodies are for the Lord, and the Lord for our bodies; and because our bodies are members of Christ, we are called to glorify God in our bodies (1 Cor. 6:13–15, 19–20). What it means to be truly human is learned as the Lord of the font frees us from the dead hands of selfdom to share the life-giving yolk of his truly human existence. As such, we never get past or move beyond our baptism, any more than Jesus does his. For the relation of baptism to the Christian life is like that of a wedding to marriage. We do not simply look back on our baptism as a major event of yesteryear, a red-letter day in the annals of life. Rather, we live out and carry forward our baptism with lifelong faith and obedience in the presence of Christ and the power of his cross and empty tomb at work in us. Indeed, baptism marks the reality of our lives forever by marking us as Christ's own. This is evident in the vows that have long accompanied baptism in the life of the church, exemplified superbly here:

> Do you renounce the devil and all the spiritual forces of wickedness that rebel against God? . . . Do you renounce the empty promises and deadly deceits of this world that corrupt and destroy the creatures of God? . . . Do you renounce the sinful desires of the flesh that draw you from the love of God? . . . Do you turn to Jesus Christ and confess him as your Lord and Savior? . . . Do you joyfully receive the Christian Faith, as revealed in the Holy Scriptures of the Old and New Testaments? . . . Will you obediently keep God's holy will and commandments, and walk in them all the days of your life?[45]

Christ and his body the church. Ethnicity, sex, and stations in life can and should be owned and duly celebrated, but only as our malformed, mythological notions of them are put to the death they so richly deserve in Christ. Anything less only lends to the racism, sexism, and classism that enthralls the world and our age. At the baptismal font we begin with unity in Christ so we can get true kingdom diversity, whereas the world starts with the diversity of its own socially constructed identities and gets not unity but endless division.

45. *The Book of Common Prayer*, Anglican Church in North America (Huntington Beach, CA: Anglican Liturgy, 2019), 164–65.

Further, we live out our baptism assured that Jesus Christ is giver of both font and feast. Baptism is the nonrepeatable sacrament of our being once-and-for-all dead to sin and alive to God through union with Christ in his death and resurrection (Rom. 6:5–11). And the Eucharist is the oft-repeated sacrament of the church being the living body of Christ, who lives in and through Christ's sustaining, sanctifying presence. The realities of the gospel do even more than resound in our ears and rinse over our bodies in the school of Christ. We taste them on our tongues and feel them in our bellies—true food and drink for true hunger and thirst. For Jesus promises quite emphatically, "Truly, truly, I say to you, unless you eat the flesh of the Son of Man and drink his blood, you have no life in you. . . . For my flesh is true food, and my blood is true drink. Whoever feeds on my flesh and drinks my blood abides in me, and I in him" (John 6:53–56). What is more, Paul tells us that our Lord's grand gospel promise is performed and punctuated in the sacrament of his body and blood: "The cup of blessing that we bless, is it not a participation in the blood of Christ? The bread that we break, is it not a participation in the body of Christ?" (1 Cor. 10:16).

After Paul testifies that the Eucharist is a participation in the body and blood of Christ, he adds that the church does this in re-membrance of Christ (1 Cor. 11:23–25). Indeed! But we must take care not to confuse remembrance with reminiscence, as if Jesus gives bread and wine only to aid our memory, our mental and emotional responses at present to things long past. Bread and wine would be ill-chosen tools for this task, because mementoes—photographs, souvenirs, heirlooms, and the like—are not meant to be eaten. Besides, participating requires real presence, whereas reminiscing requires real absence. Paul's point, therefore, is that participating in Christ is precisely the context in which we remember Christ. For as Christ makes himself present to the church through the Eucharist, the head of the body repeatedly and progressively *re-members* us, deepening and strengthening our union with him. The Eucharist could only evoke the grief and gloom of a funeral if what we presume to do is merely memorialize the broken body and shed blood of our crucified Lord in his absence—if, as Richard Hooker describes, we "account of this sacrament but only as of a shadow, destitute, empty and void of Christ."[46] Yet the Eucharist is in truth a great thanksgiving, a joyous celebration where, in the bountiful *presence* of our risen and exalted Christ, the church is warmly invited to taste and see that the Lord is good!

The Spirit seizes on the elements of bread and wine to lift the church into the presence of the Father through the Son so that we may feed on Christ in our hearts by faith with thanksgiving. In the school of Christ, our Lord has us ingest and imbibe the promises of God to palpably sign and seal in us the profoundest reality of the gospel: that our sinful bodies are made clean by his body; that our souls are washed by his most precious blood; and that we now and evermore dwell in him and he in us.[47] The chief glory of the gospel is that the gospel gives us Christ. For it is through the gospel that Christ makes himself one with believers, so that together as one body the church partakes of "this mystery, which is Christ in you, the hope of glory" (Col. 1:27; cf. John 14:20; 15:5; 17:20–23). Only by participating in Christ do we receive Christ's benefits, sharing in his very life as the incarnate Son of the Father. So our Lord gives us a most intimate and vivid realization of this mystery in the Eucharist, that visible Word of God, which is the gospel in our hands, in our mouths, and in our stomachs. The Eucharist is the sign and seal of incorporation by eating, teaching us *whose* we are and thus *who* we are—indeed, teaching us that our bodies and the body of the church are to conform to and bear the image of that most blessed fare of the holy feast: the body of Christ. Do we truly receive Christ? Truly. By what means? The gospel through faith. By what power? The Spirit. On all counts, the same is true for salvation and the Eucharist, because the Eucharist is a sacrament of the gospel, a sign and seal of our salvation, of the

---

46. Richard Hooker, *Laws of Ecclesiastical Polity* 5.67.2, in *The Works of That Learned and Judicious Divine Mr. Richard Hooker* (Oxford: Clarendon, 1865), 2:349.
47. *The Book of Common Prayer*, 119.

mystery that is Christ in us. Accordingly, Calvin extols, "It would be extreme madness to recognize no communion of believers with the flesh and blood of the Lord, which the apostle declares to be so great that he prefers to marvel at it rather than to explain it."[48]

Worship: The Epiphany of the Church and Her Theologians

Theological formation in the school of Christ is structured around Scripture and the sacraments infused by the power of the Spirit and saturated in worship. For to know God is to love God, and to love God is to worship God. In fact, true knowledge of God has its proper beginning and end in true worship of God; thus worship is not an optional add-on to knowing God but the holiest, wisest, and surest expression of it. In the unique context and calling of the church, we receive the modes of discerning, the forms of thinking and speaking, and the structures of understanding needed to grasp and articulate true knowledge of God. Renewed and transformed by the Christ who speaks and acts in his church, we are freed from the patterns and powers of this world, so that we may love and desire what God wills to make known to us. This is why the church has birthed so great a company of faithful, fruitful theologians through the centuries, all holding in common, together with Christ, deep affection for his body. And this is why immersion in the life and ministry of the church shall ever remain a mark of *every* Christian who is earnest about answering Jesus's call to theological formation.

How could it be otherwise? For theological formation in the school of Christ is saturated in worship, and worship is the triune God's gift to the church of participating by the Spirit in the incarnate Son's communion with the Father.[49] How fitting: the ultimate theologian is the ultimate worshiper! Jesus Christ is our only mediator and true high priest, the object and leader of our worship—the One we worship and the One in whom, through whom, and with whom we

---

48. Calvin, *Inst.* 4.17.9.
49. Torrance, *Worship, Community and the Triune God of Grace*, 20.

worship the Father. He teaches us to pray in his name as he inter-cedes in ours, because the Father always hears him (John 11:41–42; 16:23–24). Likewise, the church's prayers are united by the action of the Spirit with the prayers of the Son, so that we may come to the Father not as beggars seeking alms but as beloved sons and daughters seeking an inheritance. And so it is with all worship in the school of Christ, including hearing and heeding the gospel, repenting of sin, heralding and receiving Christ in Scripture and sacrament, binding ourselves to the church's faith in creed and confession, loving and serving the church and the world, catechizing, praising, lamenting, and all else beside. Jesus Christ gathers up the worship of his body, sanctifies it in himself, and offers it to the Father with his own, as his own. Worship is the epiphany of the church and her theologians, because worship manifests our conformity to the image of Christ, the ultimate theologian and worshiper. James B. Torrance writes, "The Church is the Church in her worship. Worship is not an op-tional extra, but is of the very life and essence of the Church. Nor is it a false groveling in the dust of the religiously minded. Man is never more truly man than when he worships God. He rises to all the heights of human dignity when he worships God, and all God's purposes in Creation and in Redemption are fulfilled in us as together in worship we are renewed in and through Christ, and in the name of Christ we glorify God."[50] Theological formation begins with, and always returns to, the church's union and communion with Christ. He is present to his church to conform us in heart, mind, and body to the reality of God. *Christ-ian* theology thus lives, breathes, and has its being in the body of Christ.

---

50. James B. Torrance, "The Place of Jesus Christ in Worship," in *Theological Foundations for Ministry: Selected Readings for a Theology of the Church in Minis-try*, ed. Ray S. Anderson (Edinburgh: T&T Clark; Grand Rapids: Eerdmans, 1979), 363.

4

Holy and Profane Worship

The Liturgical Cadence of Christian Theology

"What is the chief end of man?" This is the famed first question of the Westminster Catechism (1647). The answer is surprisingly brief, yet striking. The chief purpose of human existence, it answers, "is to glorify God and enjoy Him forever." The divines of Westminster were not attempting to be novel, and certainly not exhaustive. Nonetheless, their words are pregnant with meaning. It is a sentence theologians of yore might have called "pithy," a terse statement that abounds with substance. The meaning is this: humans were created with the *express* purpose of delighting in God; we live our lives according to our design and fulfill our destiny when, and only when, we do that. Indeed, that is the reason why God created the universe. The world came into being as an expression of God the Father's delight in his Son in the fellowship of the Holy Spirit; it is a world willed into existence by that triune love in order that God might share his delight with what he creates, and especially with *whom* he creates. The world is the place God has created to manifest his overflowing triune love to those other than himself. And the crown of his creation, humans, are the primary beneficiaries. Creation is a gift from God, and humans have been designed and destined to know him, rejoice in him, trust in him, and image him. In short, the universe came into existence that we might worship and glorify God, delighting in him now and forever.

Humans were created to worship God, which is to say that we were fashioned by the breath of God to have communion and fellowship with him. We exist in order that we might experience the three-personal intimacy of God in such a way that we would see and know all things in accordance with the reality of God. The primary context in which we experience our divinely ordained purpose as human creatures, as the previous chapter discussed, is the gathering of the saints in the church. That is surely why John Calvin wrote, "For it is an instance of the inestimable grace of God, that so far as the infirmity of our flesh will permit, we are lifted up even to God by the exercises of religion. What is the design of the preaching of the word, the sacraments, the holy assemblies, and the whole external government of the church, but that we may be united to God?"[1]

The purpose of worship and the purpose of humankind are the very same thing: communion with God in Christ. We fulfill and realize this destiny when we experience the end for which worship is given: sharing in the life of God. We may describe human beings in myriad ways, but a most telling definition is that the human is *Homo adorans*, "the worshiping being." If the existence of Jesus Christ shall prove anything to us, it is that God wills to be one with us, and that he will stop at nothing to make us one with him. Worship exists to manifest that divine will. "Worship," as Joseph

1. John Calvin, *Calvin's Commentaries*, Calvin Translation Society (Edinburgh, 1844–56; reprinted in 22 vols., Grand Rapids: Baker Books, 2003), 4:409–10, on Ps. 24:7. Calvin made clear elsewhere that the whole point of human existence is to know God: "Besides, if all men are born and live to the end that they may know God, . . . it is clear that all those who do not direct every thought and action in their lives to this goal degenerate from the law of their creation" (*Inst.* 1.3.3). For Calvin, to *know* God never means less than union and communion *with* God. It is high time that scholarly interpretations of Calvin acknowledge and highlight this fundamental aspect of his theology.

Cardinal Ratzinger put it, "that is, the right kind of . . . relationship with God, is essential for the right kind of human existence in the world. . . . Worship gives us a share in heaven's mode of existence, in the world of God, and allows light to fall from that divine world into ours."[2]

Once we grasp the essential nature of worship for human existence, we are in a good place to understand the essential meaning of liturgy. The term *liturgy* is bound to conjure a host of competing, confused, and contested conceptions, depending in large part on one's church background. And so we consider it salutary to offer an attempt at defining what liturgy entails, both for those who find liturgy laudable and perhaps especially for those who may find it lamentable. The liturgy of the church is the way in which the saints, with joy and awe, respond to God's self-revealing and self-giving in Christ with that most authentic of all human expressions: worship. The church's liturgy is a *theological manifestation* of her recognition that everything in heaven and on earth has been created by and for the Word of God, the only-begotten and eternally beloved Son, in whom all things hold together. As such, the church's liturgical reasoning and practice orient her—in heart, mind, and body; in prayer, confession, and song; in days, seasons, and feasts—to the holy rhythm of God's all-encompassing purpose for creation in Christ. Liturgy, in short, is the way the church "does" her deepest theological convictions.[3]

James K. A. Smith puts the above words into concise expression by noting that liturgies "shape and constitute our identities by forming our most fundamental desires and our most basic attunement to the world. In short, liturgies make us certain kinds of people, and what

2. Joseph Cardinal Ratzinger, *The Spirit of the Liturgy*, trans. John Saward (San Francisco: Ignatius, 2000), 21.

3. Frank C. Senn writes: "Liturgy (*leitourgia*) is the public work performed by a particular community under the leadership of its liturgists (*leitourgoi*) to enact its view of reality and commitments." *Christian Liturgy: Catholic and Evangelical* (Minneapolis: Fortress, 1997), xiv. The world, we must add, is full of liturgists, who enact liturgies both holy and profane.

defines us is what we *love*."[4] Liturgy, therefore, has a twofold purpose: it *shapes* our deepest, God-given purpose (to love and worship God), and it *expresses* that purpose by what we think, say, and do. That is what liturgy is all about. David Fagerberg's definition is thus profound and provocative: "Liturgy is doing the world the way the world was meant to be done."[5] Liturgy "does" the world the way it was meant to be done because it instructs us how to do it and then gives it living expression. In this most basic sense, liturgy is not at all rare or novel. Quite the contrary, it is a basic and fundamental aspect of *all* human existence—it means living with the grain of the universe God has fashioned. Humans are always and everywhere "doing" the world the way we think it ought to be done. Liturgy is not an optional human exercise; it is intrinsic and innate to our human constitution. Even if we are not always entirely conscious of it, we always live in the world according to how we understand reality. Liturgies may be heavenly or secular, they may be holy or profane, but liturgy is a given in all human life. We cannot avoid being liturgical, because we cannot avoid being worshipers: worshiping beings are and must be liturgical beings. So the question before us is never *whether* Christians will be liturgical; the question is whether that liturgy expresses reality as it is revealed and known in Christ Jesus.[6]

The way we order our lives corresponds to a basic assumption we have about what is most real. That "order" expresses—again, whether or not we are completely conscious if it—some of the most basic assumptions we possess. We live in particular, ritualized ways because

---

4. James K. A. Smith, *Desiring the Kingdom: Worship, Worldview, and Cultural Formation*, Cultural Liturgies 1 (Grand Rapids: Baker Academic, 2009), 25 (emphasis original).

5. David W. Fagerberg, *Consecrating the World: On Mundane Liturgical Theology* (Kettering, OH: Angelico, 2016), 4. Fagerberg credits this phrasing to his teacher Aidan Kavanagh, who observes, "A liturgy of Christians is . . . nothing less than the way a redeemed world is, so to speak, done." *On Liturgical Theology* (New York: Pueblo, 1984), 100.

6. In somewhat understated fashion, then, Senn states: "The distinction commonly made between 'liturgical' churches and 'nonliturgical' churches is not helpful." *Christian Liturgy*, 4.

we have particular beliefs about reality. The purpose of theology is to form our minds and hearts in accordance with the truth of Christ Jesus, who is the Alpha and Omega of all authentic human existence, so that we may live in accordance with all he is and all he has done. Liturgy is simply the way Christians express their most basic convictions about what is most true. "The purpose of all Christian liturgy," writes Robert Taft, "is to express in a ritual moment that which should be the basic stance of every moment of our lives."[7] Put this way, it is not difficult to see the direct relationship between theology and liturgy. Theology is the holy expression of reality as it is given in Christ, and liturgy is the living, worshipful enactment of that reality. "What the church should guard against," Simon Chan rightfully warns, "is a secondary theology that is done outside of the worshiping community, a theology that abstracts from and generalizes about the liturgy based on some supposedly 'neutral' criteria."[8]

Even our deepest theological convictions are ultimately empty if they do not come to concrete expression in the life of the church. Profession and practice are meant to be inextricable; the two are designed to be held together. It has been a perennial temptation for the people of God to separate the two, assuming that the theological convictions we hold can be so privatized and "spiritualized" that they end up having no obvious and direct bearing on how we order our day-to-day lives. The result is that many Christians who have orthodox *beliefs* may live unorthodox *lives*. In other words, our theological convictions may correspond to the way things really are, but the way we "do the world" may not. The Christian liturgical tradition is the primary way that the church has sought to overcome this false and unfounded dichotomy between theology and everyday life. Liturgy is a way to protect and consecrate the life of the church as she lives in the world

7. Robert Taft, "Sunday in the Eastern Tradition," in *Beyond East and West: Problems in Liturgical Understanding* (Washington, DC: Pastoral Press, 1984), 32, quoted in Fagerberg, *Consecrating the World*, 4.

8. Simon Chan, *Liturgical Theology: The Church as Worshiping Community* (Downers Grove, IL: IVP Academic, 2006), 51.

as a citizen of heaven. Liturgy seeks to do life according to Christ, theologically orienting Christians to an all-encompassing life in him. Without this orientation, the church can be seduced by and become captive to a host of competing liturgies embedded in culture—that is, alternative notions of life and reality that subtly yet incessantly seek to divert, distort, and diminish the desires of Christ's bride. Christians are called to delight in the liturgical cadence of Christian theological formation, a formation that provides holistic existence in the reality of God's design for creation. So called and formed, we are then able to uncover the persistent and pervasive expressions of liturgy and worship that seek to blunt our God-given purpose: "To glorify God and enjoy Him forever."

Sacred Liturgy

Christian liturgy is a way of recognizing that a new time has been introduced into the world through Jesus Christ. God entered the world in and through Christ, and he did not leave the time of the world unchanged. A new creation has begun right in the midst of the old one. "Therefore, if anyone is in Christ, he is a new creation. The old has passed away; behold, the new has come" (2 Cor. 5:17). It is just this kind of theological conviction that compelled the church to rethink time according to a new reality. Jesus baptized the old creation into his death and gave it a new existence in his resurrection, and so Christians were compelled to see the world in a new way. "In the light of this experience of death and resurrection time is no longer experienced merely as the hours passing and the years sliding by. The hours of the day and the seasons of the year are experienced as purposeful. The faithful perceive the times and seasons as charged with God's purposes."[9]

The church's liturgy is a way of theologically sanctifying the time of a fallen world that has experienced an all-encompassing redemp-

---

9. Frank C. Senn, *Introduction to Christian Liturgy* (Minneapolis: Fortress, 2012), 76.

tion in Jesus Christ. Whether on a micro level (the church's Sunday worship) or on a macro level (the church's existence on every other day), liturgy is a living out of the confession that Jesus Christ is the full truth of both heaven and earth: "For by him all things were created, in heaven and on earth, visible and invisible, whether thrones or dominions or rulers or authorities—all things were created through him and for him. And he is before all things, and in him all things hold together" (Col. 1:16–17). This revelation of the truth of God's purpose for all creation joyfully compels the church to "embrace with her worship the whole range of social existence in a new way, and to stamp upon ordinary human activities the imprint of Christian doctrines and ideas."[10] The church, in other words, buoyed and invigorated by the new reality revealed in and through Christ, was never able to see the world the same way again. Jesus changed everything. He did so not by obliterating the world he had first created but by sanctifying that world in accordance with God's original purpose. As Alexander Schmemann notes, a new time descended on the old: "On the day of Pentecost the Holy Spirit—and with him and in him the *new time*—descended onto the Church. The old time did not disappear, and outside in the world nothing changed. But to the Church of Christ, which lives in the Spirit and by the Spirit, the commandment and the power to convert it into the *new time* was given. 'Behold, I make all things new' (Rev. 21:5). . . . For the essence of the liturgy consists in raising us up in the Holy Spirit and in him transfiguring the old time into the new time."[11] The Spirit acquaints us with Christ, making us one with him. With and in Christ, who is the New Creation, we are given a time that is defined by him. The time in which the bride of Christ exists happens *in* the fallen world, but it is not *of* the fallen world. Christians are certainly inhabitants

---

10. Dom Gregory Dix, *The Shape of the Liturgy*, new ed. (1945; repr., London: Bloomsbury T&T Clark, 2017), 319.

11. Alexander Schmemann, *The Eucharist: Sacrament of the Kingdom*, trans. Paul Kachur (Crestwood, NY: St. Vladimir's Seminary Press, 1987), 219 (emphasis original).

of the earth, but they are *citizens* of heaven. This new citizenship requires a new kind of time and space, in which the earth is brought into heaven.

The church attempts to liturgically and worshipfully bring earth into relation with heaven precisely because her Lord has already done so. It was Jesus himself who took the world he created and made it both captivated by and captive to the Truth. By experiencing death on a Roman cross on an otherwise "normal" Friday, Jesus took that Friday and crucified it, *cruci-forming* it into a Friday unlike any the world has known. It is certainly true that every Friday already belonged to Jesus—he created them all—but he consecrated this particular Friday, etching it into the hearts of all who believe in him. The church thus commemorates this day as Good Friday, in recognition that this Friday had been taken up into the life of God in a particular and unique manner. We can now do this day "the way it was meant to be done." Christians have never seen this day the same way since, and so we honor it accordingly. That holy Friday, in turn, gave birth to a hallowed Sunday, which Jesus sanctified once and for all by making this last day of creation the first day of a new creation. By vanquishing death on Sunday, Jesus took that day and made it his own, breaking the bonds of its longtime corruption and distortion. The "day of the Sun" became the "day of the Son," as he resurrected a fallen creation into the light of his Father's kingdom time. The last day of the week became both the first and eighth day of the week, the Alpha and Omega of sanctified time. Christ made Sunday a liberated captive to his resurrection, elevating it into the time of his Father's kingdom. Christians have never seen this day the same way since, and so we honor it accordingly. This Sunday became for the church Easter Sunday or Resurrection Sunday, in honor of our Lord rising from the dead. Time became theologized.

Good Friday and Easter Sunday are but two prominent examples of the way the church liturgically lives out her deepest theological commitments, the crucifixion and resurrection of the Lord Jesus. But the church also realizes that two days could not possibly pay proper homage to the way Jesus reorients time. After all, what about the birth of Jesus? Or his baptism? Or his transfiguration? Or his sending of the Holy Spirit on the day of Pentecost? Or his ascension to the right hand of God the Father almighty? These too are time-altering events that shook reality to its core. So it is no wonder that Christians sought to bring these redemptive events to bear on a calendar that needed sanctifying. And so days, months, and seasons came under the impress of Jesus, the Lord of creation and time. The church decided to live her life theologically, framing time in concert with the all-encompassing gospel of Christ. The rhythmical seasons God gave to the world—winter, spring, summer, and fall—did not cease to exist for the faithful. Rather, they became reinterpreted in the light of Christ as seasons of Advent, Epiphany, Lent, Easter, and Pentecost. The seasons were theologically "Christened" to reflect who Christ is and what he has done. Seasons were "Christened," but so were days. Otherwise mundane days become sacred days: the church consecrated specific days to commemorate the Lord's birth, his baptism, his annunciation, his transfiguration, and his ascension, to name a few. A Christian liturgical calendar is nothing more or less than a sanctified attempt to theologize time in accordance with the revelation of Christ.

Spending Our Lives

One of the most important ways that theology orients us to reality is by referring our everyday experiences to the truth of God's revelation. Tish Harrison Warren has memorably encapsulated this truth: "If I am to spend my whole life being transformed by the good news of Jesus, I must learn how grand, sweeping truths—doctrine, theology, ecclesiology, Christology—rub against the texture of an average day. How I spend this ordinary day in Christ is how I will spend my Christian life."[12] The fundamental confession of the church—that

12. Tish Harrison Warren, *Liturgy of the Ordinary: Sacred Practices in Everyday Life* (Downers Grove, IL: InterVarsity, 2016), 24. Warren is reflecting on a quote from

everything in heaven and earth has been created by, through, and for Jesus Christ—means we are liberated to conceive of all things in a new way. We are not constrained to conceive of the world on its own terms. This is impossible, because the world is created by God and so has no self-referential or self-explanatory basis from which it can be understood. Secularism, notes Schmemann, is a lie about the world. It is an attempt to "live in the world as if there were no God!" Christian liturgy, he adds, "*demands* exactly the opposite: to live in the world seeing *everything* in it as a revelation of God, a sign of His presence, the joy of His coming, the call to communion with Him, the hope for fulfillment in Him. Since the day of Pentecost there is a seal, a ray, a sign of the Holy Spirit on everything for those who believe in Christ and know that He is the life of the world—and that in Him the world in its totality has become again a *liturgy*, a *communion*, an *ascension*."[13] Creation can be properly conceived only in relation to its Creator. And herein lies the basis for all authentic Christian thought: In Jesus Christ, and *only* in Jesus Christ, Creator and creature have been united—heaven and earth have been joined together. In Jesus, earth has been brought into relation to heaven in such a way that what was created can hereafter only be properly conceived in relation to the One by whom and for whom creation exists. Conceptions of reality that do not bow before the reality of Jesus Christ, as we have previously noted, are nothing more than abstractions, ideas pulled away from reality. Such conceptions attempt to deal with the world on its own terms, blind to the fact that Jesus is the full reality of the Creator and the full reality of all that God has created.

The world was created to be lived theologically—in a sharp and settled awareness that what God has created relies entirely on God for its meaning. Because *nothing* is entirely self-referential or self-existent except God, creation demands definition. And that defi-

---

Annie Dillard: "How we spend our days is, of course, how we spend our lives." *The Writing Life* (New York: Harper & Row, 1989), 32.

13. Alexander Schmemann, *For the Life of the World: Sacraments and Orthodoxy*, 2nd ed. (Crestwood NY: St. Vladimir's Seminary Press, 2002), 112 (emphasis original).

nition must come from God. The most poignant and arresting demonstration of this theological axiom is the teaching of our Lord in the Gospel of John. A rather large part of John's Gospel is a witness to Jesus's determined effort to theologize—indeed, liturgize—the world he created. What John learned from his Lord was that the world we inhabit is suffused with theological significance. The opening of John's Gospel is striking testimony to the apostle's theological and liturgical renaissance. "In the beginning was the Word, and the Word was with God, and the Word was God. He was in the beginning with God. All things were made through him, and without him was not any thing made that was made" (John 1:1–3). The English translation of this passage may blunt the force of John's *intended provocation*, given that the Greek term *logos*—Word—was freighted with philosophical and ideological significance in Greco-Roman culture. *Logos* was understood as the underlying rational, logical, and noetic principle that lends order and meaning, truth and reality, to the universe. What John does with the term *logos* is paradigm-altering and jaw-dropping, to say the least.[14] *Logos*, as it was commonly understood, was too transcendent a concept to be embodied in a human being, too heavenly a notion to be defined in terms of Jesus of Nazareth, the simple son of a simple carpenter. Yet John came to know that the logic behind all logic, the reason governing all other reason, the *Word* that orders and defines all truth and reality is none other than Jesus of Nazareth, the divine *Logos* become fully human. John woke from his mundane slumber and was evermore at pains to proclaim the earth-altering revelation that without Jesus not one thing came into being, so not one thing can be properly conceived *apart* from him.

14. It is a common misconception that the early church borrowed from Greek philosophy in an effort to elucidate the gospel. Far from it. In addition to John's use of *logos*, the church's use of *homoousion*, for example, would have horrified the philosophers. James B. Torrance writes: "What could be more un-Hellenic than the statement of the Creed that God 'was made man'!" "The Vicarious Humanity of Christ," in *The Incarnation: Ecumenical Studies in the Nicene-Constantinopolitan Creed A.D. 381*, ed. Thomas F. Torrance (Eugene, OR: Wipf & Stock, 1998), 132.

John's Gospel goes on to describe how Jesus interprets one earthly experience after another in theological terms, opening our eyes to see the everyday world as pregnant with the Truth, allowing us to see the world as a grand and divinely ordained liturgy. It begins at the wedding at Cana, where Jesus turns water into wine (John 2). The fruit of the vine had always been understood by Israel as a sign of God's abundant provision and blessing. What Jesus does by turning six jars of water into well over a hundred gallons of wine is to show that he is the true vine of God's people, the One who would truly "gladden the heart of man" (Ps. 104:15). Jesus takes an assumption about what wine meant and interprets it in terms of himself—he becomes the *logos* (logic) of wine. The same is true of water. Jesus's encounter with the Samaritan woman at the well marks a heavenly reinterpretation of the meaning of H_2O. This woman knows she needs water for living, but she does not yet know she needs Jesus, the living water (John 4:10). He allows her to see through the water to its theological meaning: the gift of water is a sign of purification and refreshment. Christ is the meaning of the water we so desire and need. The same logic (*logos*) applies to the bread that humanity longs for and lives by. After Jesus miraculously multiplies fish and loaves to satisfy the appetites of the crowds, he is quick to insist that what they truly long for is bread from heaven (John 6). The meaning of their hunger is his own flesh and blood, which alone can truly make them eternally full. He challenges the crowds to see through food to its theological meaning: the gift of God's life-giving sustenance in Christ. Christ is the meaning of the bread for which we long. The same applies to the experience of the temple, a building rife with the promise of God to dwell with his people. Jesus identifies his own body as the *logos* of the temple, the true place where God dwells with man. Jesus is the meaning of the temple, the specific and precise location of God's dwelling with his people: God dwells with and in us through Christ, who is himself the tabernacle and temple of God (John 3:18–22).

Christ liturgizes and theologizes the world by taking the material "stuff" of creation and filling out its meaning.[15] But he also takes our ideational assumptions captive to himself, giving them a basis in reality they could not have without him. A striking and stirring example of this comes from Jesus's encounter with Martha after the death of her brother Lazarus. Jesus consoles Martha with the words "Your brother will rise again." Martha's response is revealing: "I know that he will rise again in the resurrection on the last day." What Jesus then says to her is an upheaval and reconfiguration of her assumption about the meaning of death, resurrection, and life: "I am the resurrection and the life. Whoever believes in me, though he die, yet shall he live, and everyone who lives and believes in me shall never die" (John 11:23–26). Notice that Jesus does not affirm her assumptions about the meaning of Lazarus's death and resurrection but rather refers that meaning to himself: "I am!" Resurrection is not a concept, Jesus insists, but a living reality defined by his personal existence as the One who is the death and life of humanity. Jesus, in other words, does not merely provide the conditions under which "resurrection" may occur for Lazarus; he is himself the reality through which Lazarus may experience life through death. Jesus takes Martha's "concept" of resurrection and gives it living reality in his own existence. He *is* the resurrection.

There is a similar reconfiguration of reality that takes place in an exchange Jesus has with his disciple Thomas. Jesus says in Thomas's hearing, "In my Father's house are many rooms. . . . And if I go and prepare a place for you, I will come again and will take you to myself,

15. Case in point: Jesus, the second Adam, takes into his holy hands the soil of the earth, subject to thorns, thistles, and all manner of futility at the hands of the first Adam (Gen. 3:17–19). Mixing that soil with his life-giving saliva, Jesus, the light of the world, then uses it to scatter the darkness of the man born blind (John 9:1–11). Here, as everywhere, Jesus transforms what he touches, remolding the cursed ground and repurposing it for healing and enlightenment. In the human hands of God the Son, even dirt is put to God's re-creative purposes for the world. What a poignant example of how Jesus "comes to make His blessings flow Far as the curse is found, Far as the curse is found" (Isaac Watts, "Joy to the World," *Hymns for the Family of God* [Nashville: Brentwood-Benson, 1976], no. 171).

that where I am you may be also. And you know the way to where I am going" (John 14:2–4). Like Martha before him, Thomas is beset by abstract concepts about the truth. Hence his request: "Lord, we do not know where you are going. How can we know the way?" (John 14:5). As with Martha, so too with Thomas—Jesus refers Thomas's preconceived assumptions about the way things are supposed to be to himself: "I am the way, and the truth, and the life. No one comes to the Father except through me" (John 14:6). Thomas needs to learn that his conceptions of the way to life must be understood entirely in relation to Christ. Jesus is not *a way* to God, nor is he an exalted and appointed *director* of that way. Jesus does not simply teach us about the way to God; he is himself that Way because he is the Truth and Life of God in himself. Apart from Jesus, there are innumerable ways of conceiving what "way," "truth," and "life" may mean. Jesus takes Thomas's abstractions and gives them concrete reality: "I am!"

Thomas needs to have his understanding of reality altered, and he comes to know that Jesus is the way to God *as that Way*, that Jesus is the truth of God *as that Truth*, and that Jesus is the life of God *as that Life*. All of this is lost on Pontius Pilate only a few chapters later when Pilate is examining Jesus's fitness for death by crucifixion. Prompted by Jesus's words, "Everyone who is of the truth listens to my voice," Pilate asks Jesus a most theologically loaded question: "What is truth?" (John 18:37–38). The irony is intended to hit the reader like a ton of bricks: Pilate has asked the Truth what truth is. Pilate's rhetorical question is calculated to silence the Truth, but instead it exposes that Pilate is working with a concept not defined by the Lord. Truth, for Pilate, is an abstraction, an erroneous notion put in the service of denying that very Truth. Pilate is unable to see through his notion of "truth" to the basis and meaning of it, even as he looks him square in the face. Pilate walks away secure in a comfort that has no basis in reality, thus playing his representative role in the crucifixion of the Truth.

This exercise in the theology of John's Gospel serves to demonstrate the manner in which Jesus "liturgized" the world. Consistently and constantly, Jesus reordered and reestablished the meaning of the world we live in by referring the most basic earthly realities to himself. Material realities like wine, water, and bread were given their meaning. Conceptions like life, death, resurrection, and truth were placed in direct relationship to him. He took the creation he fashioned and reconciled it with God, directing creation to its ultimate meaning and destiny. In so doing, Jesus was uniting heaven and earth by uniting God and man, bringing the two into a perfect union. He gave us the vision to see the world the way it was meant to be seen, giving us the ability to "do the world the way it was meant to be done." In Christ, the world became theologically electrified with a new reality. The liturgy of the church, to put it simply, is the way we live in this reality.

Symbolical and Diabolical

By uniting creation with its Creator, Jesus has become the great Sacrament (Greek, *mysterion*) of God and the world. He is, after all, the visible image of the invisible God—holding all things in heaven and earth together in himself (Col. 1:15–17). Jesus is the ultimate liturgist, conforming the world to its divinely ordained design. Whereas Western theology has typically referred to Jesus as the true *Sacrament* (Latin, *Sacramentum*), Eastern theology has often preferred the term *symbol* to refer to Jesus's theological task. The English term *symbol* derives from the ancient Greek word *symballein*, which means quite literally to "throw together." Jesus unites heaven and earth by throwing it together (symbolizing it). He gives earth meaning by joining it to heaven. He gives creation meaning by joining it to the Creator. Most importantly, though, he gives us meaning by joining us to God. To put this transcendent truth in theological shorthand, Christians confess that the *Word became flesh*. By becoming what he created, God the Word (*Theos-Logos*) did not cease to be perfectly God; rather, he took what he created into sacramental and symbolical union with himself. He brought what he created into a grand and all-encompassing testimony to himself, so that the creation could be lived in light of reality. In Christ Jesus, the world became a holy liturgy again. At her very most vibrant and joyful, the church has attempted to spend her life in the way, truth, and life of Christ—the One who gives meaning to the days, months, and seasons, which exist for his glory.

Sundays became different, as did Fridays. Spring took on a whole new meaning, as did fall. Even the setting and rising of the sun became impossible to conceive of apart from the setting of the Son into a death from which he rose again. The most important of our earthly experiences became liturgical and theological. The meaning of childbirth became impregnated with the nativity of our Lord; the meaning of marriage became solemnized in the union between Christ and his church; the meaning of hunger and thirst became consumed with the significance of Christ's flesh and blood; the meaning of death and life became flooded with the import of Christ's baptism. Reality became embedded and embodied in the person and work of the One who holds all things together.

Theology has a liturgical cadence and context because it seeks to express reality in the everyday life of the Christian. Theology expresses itself liturgically in the sense that it seeks to "hold together" the reality of the Creator and the reality of creation, instilling the latter with the former. Living liturgically is nothing less or other than living theologically, which is to say, living according to our deepest convictions. We must acknowledge, however, that Christians are often tempted to live in a liturgy that does not coincide with their deepest theological convictions. Instead of spending our lives in a world where heaven and earth have been "thrown together" (*symballein*), the church may be tempted to live in a world that has been "thrown apart" (*diaballein*).[16] Instead of living *symbolically*, the church may be enticed to live *diabolically*. Christians will live liturgically either

16. For this highly instructive Greek wordplay we are indebted to Fagerberg, *Consecrating the World*, 85–86.

way, because every last human being is created to be a worshiper (*Homo adorans*), and worshiping beings are necessarily liturgical beings. The nature and form of that liturgy, however, will depend on whether it is conformed to a world held together or a world torn asunder.

Profane Liturgy

Martin Luther once referred to the devil as a "master of a thousand arts," aware as he was that the devil has his own theological and liturgical designs on humanity.[17] Luther knew that the Word of God was the ultimate theologian and liturgist, but that did not mean that Christ was the only one. The devil, too, seeks to theologize and liturgize humanity toward a reality of his own making. For Luther, the question was never *whether* people would be taught to live worshipfully; the question was rather *by whom*. If the people of God refuse to be formed by the Word of God, they will be formed to live under the tutelage of a diabolical adjunct, who has his own theology and liturgy. Unlike Jesus, who holds together the things of earth with the things of heaven, the devil is a master of tearing them apart. His diabolical liturgy is characterized by its attempt to curve the world in on itself rather than opening the world up to the reality of its meaning in Christ Jesus. If sacred theology begets sacred liturgy, then just as surely profane theology begets profane liturgy.[18] Jesus intends for us to "do the world the way it was meant to be done." So does the devil. To massively understate the case, each has very different understandings of how the world is meant to be done.

Broaching the topic of the devil brings to mind the words of C. S. Lewis's imaginary interlocutor: "Do you really mean, at this time of day, to re-introduce our old friend the devil—hoofs and horns and

---

17. Martin Luther's preface to *The Large Catechism*, in *BC*, 381.
18. We use the term *profane* in its literal sense—that is, treating something irreverently that is designed to be holy. This is different from mere vulgarity. Something is profane if and when it fails to recognize that which is holy.

all?"[19] That many in the church continue, in our day, to entertain a comically naive notion of Satan, that pointy-tailed, trident-toting lord of the fiery underworld, is no laughing matter. A devil rendered comical is only minimally dangerous, because he lacks subtlety. But it is precisely his subtlety that is dangerous.[20] The enlightened minds of some moderns may be reticent to admit the influence of the devil when it comes to how we live in the world, but we need not entertain laughable notions of the diabolical to see that our lives are too often indistinguishable from those who do not confess that Jesus has transformed reality. If Jesus has taken the life of the world up into the life of God, then living in the world as if it were self-explanatory—as if the world were capable on its own merits of providing the inner resources for reality—would be to live diabolically and not theologically. The problem with "worldly" living is not the world per se; the problem arises when we attempt to live in the world created and redeemed by Christ as if it were self-referential. "The world becomes worldly when it becomes our end, and not means; the world becomes worldly when it is not a sacramental sign of heaven; the world becomes worldly when it is not put on a liturgical trajectory."[21]

And yet it is crucial to recognize that there is more than one liturgical trajectory on offer in the world. There is a liturgy that exists in reference to the melody of Christ, and there are innumerable liturgies set to different tunes. Because humans are invariably worshipers, they are inescapably theological and liturgical. Everyone attempts to rhythmically measure life according to how reality is conceived. This holds true for the church no less than for the world, believer and nonbeliever alike. Living liturgically is not in the least unique, as if it were an enclave particular to the "religiously serious." Liturgies are

19. C. S. Lewis, *Mere Christianity*, rev. and exp. ed. (New York: HarperOne, 2015), 46.

20. This passage is excerpted from Marcus Peter Johnson, "Who's Your Teacher? Our Sacred Duty to Teach the Devil to Death," *Touchstone: A Journal of Mere Christianity* 28, no. 5 (September/October 2015): 15–17.

21. Fagerberg, *Consecrating the World*, 46.

ubiquitous. They exist whenever and wherever people attempt to live in the truth as they perceive it. In that sense, liturgies may be Christian or secular, holy or profane. Either way, as Smith notes, liturgies seek to form and transform the deepest desires of humankind. "'Secular' liturgies are fundamentally formative, and implicit in them is a vision of the kingdom that needs to be discerned and evaluated. From the perspective of Christian faith, these secular liturgies will often constitute a *mis*-formation of our desires—aiming our heart away from the Creator to some aspect of the creation as if it were God. Secular liturgies capture our hearts by capturing our imaginations and drawing us into ritual practices that 'teach' us to love something very different from the kingdom of God."[22] Liturgies may be described as "profane" when they seek to orient people—through the rousing of imagination, the stirring of desire, the awakening of love, the practicing of habits, the disciplining of our wills, the spending of time—to a reality that is not defined by the reality of God in Christ. Such liturgies are by no means in short supply, and they are not all necessarily wicked, but they are certainly pervasive, powerful, elaborate, sophisticated, and rather well thought out. Worshipers are very careful in the way they worship, and they tend to leave no detail unattended, because there is nothing that does not mean *something*. The *Homo adorans* is always in search of a liturgy to express the truth. "That is why," Ratzinger observes, "there are in reality no societies altogether lacking in cult. Even the decidedly atheistic, materialistic systems create their own forms of cult, though, of course, they can only be an illusion and strive in vain, by bombastic trumpeting, to conceal their nothingness."[23]

It is high time for the church to come to grips with a crippling dichotomous assumption that is regnant in contemporary life and

---

22. Smith, *Desiring the Kingdom*, 88. Smith uses the term *secular* loosely, seeing that all humans are "liturgical animals." Even so, the distinction between secular and sacred can be—and often is—overwrought. Both Christian and non-Christian liturgies are ever and always expressions of worship.

23. Ratzinger, *Spirit of the Liturgy*, 21.

discourse—that there is a cultural and anthropological divide between those who are "religious" and those who are not. This is entirely false. The real cultural divide is, in fact, between varying *performances* of religion. "Atheism" is an oxymoron. Everyone is a "theist" for the very reason that everyone is driven by an ultimate love (and fear) of some transcendent reality. All people are theologians; all people are worshipers; and thus all people are liturgical. When we are awakened to this stubborn and ineluctable fact, we are in a far better position to heed the holy caution of John: "Beloved, do not believe every spirit, but test the spirits to see whether they are from God" (1 John 4:1). There are innumerable "spirits" on offer, but there is all the difference in heaven and earth between the spirit of our age and the *Spirit of our Lord*. The former tethers us to a world that is passing away; the latter tethers us to Jesus Christ, who is the end of all religion and the beginning of true worship. Testing the zeitgeist has never been a simple task for the church, not in John's time or ours. The difficulty resides in the biblical truth that we Christians are called to live in a world in which we do not exactly belong.

If the church is ever forgetful that humans are designed to "do the world" according to Christ, the world is happy to fill that liturgical void. Absent the God-given liturgy of Word and sacrament—of faith and repentance; of baptism and Supper; of songs, prayers, and creeds; of holy days and holy nights—the world will gladly provide a plethora of alternatives. Why? Because humanity is incurably and inescapably liturgical. The most "successful" alternatives to explicitly Christian liturgical life are the ones most parasitic on the genuine article. The cult of athletics provides us with a poignant example. The religious zealousness of sports enthusiasts is both propagated and cultivated by its rather complex and obvious liturgical character. It does not take a seasoned theologian to see that major sporting events have their own unique, but never original, liturgical elements. To attend such an event, one enters an elaborate and ornate stadium (temple) built on the sacrificial generosity (tithing) of its benefactors. Attendees bear witness to their allegiance with the jerseys and uniforms (vestments) of their heroes. Children are initiated (baptized) into the ritual, witnesses to the great joy their parents educate (catechize) them into, prepared at home to anticipate the great event. They too are clothed with the garments of the conquerors. Food is eaten (Supper), invocations are plentiful (prayer), songs are sung (praise). People are ecstatic because the concert of human fellowship (Greek, *koinonia*) is intoxicating. The closer one is seated to the main event, the more sacred is the experience (altar and sanctuary). People are directed to rhythmically sit and rise in fidelity to the planned script (order of worship). Lengthy and costly travel is commonplace (pilgrimage), and devotees are sent forth (Latin, *missio*; "massed") into the world to proclaim the good news (gospel) of their experience.

Every last aspect of the sporting event is calculated to arouse and satisfy the appetite of the congregants in heart and mind, body and soul. But it becomes insatiable by design. Sunday devotion is never enough. The meal must be extended to Saturday, and then Monday night, and then even Thursday. Whole weeks and months— "championship week" and "March Madness"—become engulfed in the liturgy. In the end, nearly every day becomes a liturgical observance in one form or another. The prevalence of the sporting liturgy is ample evidence that people desire, and are committed, to spend their day-to-day lives in what brings them the greatest joy. And that is what makes this liturgy, or any other non-Christian liturgy, entirely unoriginal. They are no more than parasitic on the basic fact that humans desire to sanctify their everyday existence. God made us to do just that.

There is nothing surprising about the existence of complex and all-encompassing liturgies that prevail in our culture. They are to be expected. The surprise is that many Christians are more familiar with these types of liturgies than they are their own Christian liturgy. The surprise is that so many in the church replace a sacred liturgy with the daily demands of alternate liturgies. It is not diabolical to attend a football game, to cite one example, but it can become diabolical when the demands of the attending liturgy begin to compete with the demands of the liturgy of the church. When the Sabbath becomes devoted to football, it marks the ascendance of one kind of worship over another.

But we need not focus on athletic liturgies to make the point. There are a host of alternate liturgies—taken separately or together—that vie for the hearts and minds of Christians, that seek to frame our conceptions of reality. And they are decidedly liturgical. A typical university education is a glaring example of a complex and committed liturgy that seeks to define reality for its congregants. Students are welcomed into a vast array of ceremonies and rituals that establish their fidelity to the university mission, including ornate vestments and initiatory rites. They are regularly and systematically catechized by sustained preaching and teaching about the meaning of life (philosophy), the meaning of the human being (anthropology, sociology), the inner life of the soul (psychology), the existence and purpose of creation (geology, natural sciences), the purpose and meaning of history (world history), and even of human worship (comparative religion) and sexuality (biology). Students study together, eat together, and sleep with one another, participating in a host of prescribed activities whose purpose is to advocate and propagate a vision for a meaningful life. Time is regulated, days and months are given strict definition, songs are sung. Universities exist in order to train their students to "do the world the way it was meant to be done." And it is all done, we are assured, without the constraints of "religion."[24] The irony is thick, to say the least, since the university provides one of the most advanced and sophisticated liturgies in existence. "The university remains a charged religious institution not (only) because of the epistemic conditions that undergird knowledge and research,

24. It is not uncommon for Christian universities and colleges to become pre-occupied with establishing connections and linkages between the Christian faith and alternate forms of defining reality. So Richard John Neuhaus cautions: "Linkages have an insidious way of turning into sponges. . . . In relating Christianity to some other way of constructing reality, the other way too often demonstrates the greater power of absorption. The result, from the Christian viewpoint, is apostasy." *Freedom for Ministry*, rev. ed. (Grand Rapids: Eerdmans, 1992), 146.

but (also) because the university is a formative, liturgical institution, animated by rituals and liturgies that constitute a pedagogy of desire. The university is not just out to deposit information in our heads with a view to professional success. . . . Rather, the university can't help but be a formative institution because of powerful (though often unofficial) liturgies that shape our identity and self-understanding."[25] The mission of the university is the same as the mission of the church: shaping the identity and self-understanding of its congregants. They are both attempting to enact reality, but with very different assumptions about what or who defines that reality. Despite their insistence to the contrary, the *last* thing universities are is "nonreligious." They are simply a particular kind of worshipful expression adorned with specialized liturgies suited to the contemporary and awakened *Homo adorans*. Christians have always known that baptism, the preaching of the truth, and holy communion are the most basic elements of human identity and self-understanding. Universities are parasitic in this regard, employing the same elements in a very different mode.

The liturgical emphases found in sporting and university life are not exceptions in the least. They sit alongside of, and often deeply coincide with, a number of other prevalent profane liturgies on offer in contemporary culture. The entertainment complex that originates in Hollywood is another example of a rather intricate ordering of reality. Through its incessant preaching and teaching, it strives to interpret the meaning of life. It employs highly regarded and decorated priests and priestesses (icons) to proclaim its gospel, constructs elaborate and extravagant liturgical celebrations that attract a hungry audience (the Oscars), and even provides a calendar for the proper observance of its virtual rituals. Hollywood may be generally dismissive of, even hostile to, the commitments of the church; but that is only because it has manufactured an alternate church replete with sanctuaries and saints that bear impressive witness to another understanding of truth.

---

25. Smith, *Desiring the Kingdom*, 112–13.

What applies to the liturgical cult of entertainment applies equally to the cult of politics, which is no less committed to shaping specific understandings of reality. The master liturgies of entertainment are matched by the liturgical mastery of politicians, who are zealous to order the desires of a people in accordance with their fundamental convictions. Political parties, ostensibly committed to the separation of church and state, nevertheless carefully indoctrinate and catechize their subjects in the basics of their respective kingdoms. Predictably, political assemblies rely on songs and creeds, lecterns and pulpits, revivals and renewals, to energize, fortify, and instruct the faithful. Indeed, political conventions are among the most detailed and measured liturgies in existence, calculated to arouse hearts and minds to doing the world in accordance with a specific understanding of reality. The political cult assumes we will spend our lives devoted to its prescribed forms of worship, even commandeering calendar days dedicated to the observance of its saints and martyrs.

By briefly describing a few of the most influential liturgies that captivate contemporary culture, we hope to unmask the naive notion that our secular age is becoming increasingly nonreligious. No. Humans are every bit as worshipful and theological as they have ever been. This miniature exercise in liturgical awareness serves to underscore the point of this chapter: our deepest theological commitments shape our understanding of reality, and they always occur in a liturgical context. The liturgies of our age may not be *theological* in the sense that they are captivated by Jesus Christ the God-Word (*Theos-Logos*), but they are most certainly religious in the sense that they assume and assert a principal authority for determining what matters most. The christological, trinitarian, ecclesial, and sacramental commitments that give shape to Christian liturgies are countered by the technological, individualistic, Gnostic, and rationalistic commitments that give shape to their alternatives.

The profane liturgies of the contemporary renaissance man are successful in large part because they appeal to those "enlightened" folk who have ostensibly transcended the need for religious ritual to define the world. Modern people, we are told, have been liberated from their vestigial, religious captivity and are no longer in need of sacred rituals to determine the meaning of life. This, we must emphatically state, *is a myth*. Such moderns may be ignorant of the Ten Commandments, but they endlessly legislate ethical norms. They may not visit a church or cathedral, but that is only because they are busy building shrines to glorify their self-interest. They may think of the intimacy between Christ and his bride as an unseemly eroticism, but they are titillated by half-naked cheerleaders at stadiums. They consider it barbaric that God would offer his only begotten Son as a sacrifice for the sins of the world but barely blush when aborted bodies of children are offered as a sacrifice to the god of fornication. They may know nothing of the sacred, life-giving symbolism of bread and wine, but only because they are consumed with the benefits of a "healthy diet" that will help them stave off death. In a quest for "wholeness," modern people replace the counsel of God's Word and the taking of the Lord's Supper with the counsel of their therapists and the taking of supplements, simply Word and sacrament of a different sort. They find *theo*-logy irrelevant and boring but *techno*-logy alluring and captivating, as evidenced by the fact that "virtual reality" is no longer understood as self-evidently oxymoronic. The Lenten preparations for Good Friday and Easter Sunday appear needless, but their preparations for Black Friday and Super Bowl Sunday are crucial. Rainbows represent for them a quaint piece of Old Testament mythology, unless of course rainbows can symbolize one's sexually liberated identity. The point, we hope, is clear: "nonreligious" and "nonliturgical" people are obsessed with religion and liturgy. They cannot help it.

Lex Orandi, Lex Credenda

Historic Christian liturgies were developed by the church in order to give theological meaning to Christian life. There were two (simultaneous) motivations for the development, one positive and the other negative. The positive development of the liturgy was motivated by a desire to *shape* the world in accordance with reality as it is given in Christ. In Word and sacrament, in prayer and praise, in song and creed, in days and months, in sight and sound and smell, a Christian liturgy "theologizes" the world according to the revelation of God in Christ. The negative development was motivated by a desire to *resist* any and all liturgies that shape the world in accordance with some other reality. The church was aware that the various alternate liturgies on offer in the world were not only present but very often regnant and thus constituted a real threat to the proper ordering of the Christian life. These embedded liturgies were, in their own fallen way, well thought out, complex, impressive, and alluring. Indeed, they could hardly be avoided. And so the church knew that it must offer to Christians a way of doing the world that accorded with the all-encompassing reality of Christ.

There is a Latin maxim that encapsulates the main point of this chapter: *lex orandi, lex credenda*, "The law of praying determines the law of believing." Theologically expanded, the phrase captures the truth that the way we worship gives shape and substance to the way we believe. Or, to put it another way, theology has a worshipful, liturgical context. "If good theology is good anything else, it is good worship."[26] Our deepest convictions and confessions arise from our experience of God in worship. Our saintly predecessors in the faith were entirely cognizant of this, and so ordered worship in a way that would breathe theological meaning into our lives. Every element of the Christian liturgy is designed to make us the kind of people who recognize reality. As we hear the Word of God, we are familiarized with the *Logos* who lies behind all logic. When we are baptized, we are given an identity that defines us forever. When we partake of the Lord's Supper, we learn the meaning of nourishment and health. When we pray, our thoughts and desires are consecrated to heaven. When we confess the creeds, we are given language to

26. Neuhaus, *Freedom for Ministry*, 147.

express the truth as it really is.[27] When we observe holy days, months, and seasons, we acknowledge that time and history belong to Jesus. In short, the liturgy of the church engages us, in body and soul, to hold reality together as it has been revealed in Christ.

For this reason, it is entirely misleading to say that most Christians have never received a formal theological education. The opposite is true. All Christians receive a (literally) *formal* theological education by way of their formative experience of the formalities of worship. That experience may be liturgically sophisticated or not, but either way Christians are theologically trained by what they hear, experience, pray, say, confess, and do as they gather to commune with God. They may leave the sanctuary with the wherewithal to see and live in the world according to Christ, or they may leave impoverished and thus susceptible to a thousand other liturgies. But let it be said forthrightly: for better or for worse, every Christian leaves the liturgy of the church a theologian in the making.

27. Neuhaus puts this wonderfully: "How many churchgoing Christians are aware that the great ecumenical creeds they recite on Sunday reflect a *theory of reality* that is comprehensive, intellectually rigorous, majestically nuanced—a theory that by comparison makes most of the regnant philosophies of our time seem like almost accidental collections of careless guesswork? Not many Christians would suspect it, in large part because they have not heard it set forth from their pulpits. Thus, Christianity remains for many an amalgam of sentiment, nostalgia, psychic uplift, and bland moralism. Many of these people suspect that there must be more to it than this." *Freedom for Ministry*, 197 (emphasis added).

The Postulate of Paradox

The Mysterious Nature of Christian Theology

In an essay penned approximately sixty years ago, Vernon Grounds advanced a provocative thesis. He wondered whether evangelicals—we might add, modern Christians generally—"are so ensnared by alien principles that we refuse to take seriously the postulate of paradox, a postulate without which evangelicalism ceases to have an evangel." His concern was that many Christians, under the influence of a logic not specifically derived from the *Logos*, have become enthralled with demonstrating the intellectual cogency of the Christian faith in a way that leaves little room for the biblical and theological significance of paradox. According to Grounds, this is a major misstep. "Instead of keeping paradox hidden from sight like a deformed imbecile of whom we are ashamed," he wrote, we ought to "welcome it proudly into the very throne-room of theology—a kind of Cinderella at long last discovered and exalted to her rightful place."[1]

As insightful and artfully posed as this thesis is, it is not nearly so novel as it may first appear. Paradox, the "deformed imbecile" of

1. Vernon C. Grounds, "The Postulate of Paradox," *Bulletin of the Evangelical Theological Society* 7, no. 1 (Winter 1964): 3.

which Grounds writes, has not always been a source of shame for Christians. If paradox and its cousin mystery are to be exalted to the throne room of theology, it will involve not so much a *discovery* as a *recovery*. Welcoming paradox proudly into our theology will require not an exercise in novelty but, rather, a jogging of our memory; for unlike Cinderella, paradox once sat enthroned.

Terms like *paradox* and *mystery* have fallen on hard times, too easily mistaken as synonyms or even scapegoats for flights into absurdity and irrationality. However, when these terms are understood in their biblical and theological context, they acknowledge that the truth and logic of God confront us with a type of knowledge that transcends our intellectual assumptions—assumptions that are not only finite but fallen. Paradox and mystery, in other words, are categories of thought that are necessary for the church because the church is the recipient of *revelation*, a disclosure of reality that comes to us from above and without, not from below and within. And so the church must once again embrace paradox and mystery as a humble acknowledgment that God's thoughts and ways are not our thoughts and ways: "As the heavens are higher than the earth, so my ways are higher than your ways and my thoughts than your thoughts" (Isa. 55:9). It is to appreciate and honor the fact that "the foolishness of God is wiser than men" (1 Cor. 1:25) and that God is indeed incomparable: "To whom then will you liken God, or what likeness compare with him?" (Isa. 40:18). The revelation of God cannot be comprehended, no less constrained, by mere human thought, wisdom, or comparison.[2]

The prophets and apostles knew that when they encountered God, they came up against a revelation that tried and tested reality as they perceived it. Time and again, they were confronted and even

2. "As the Greek Fathers insisted, 'A God who is comprehensible is not God.' A God, that is to say, whom we claim to understand exhaustively through the resources of our reasoning brain turns out to be no more than an idol, fashioned in our own image." Kallistos Ware, *The Orthodox Way* (Crestwood, NY: St. Vladimir's Seminary Press, 1993), 13.

bewildered by a God who shattered their mundane expectations. Their wisdom had to be shown foolish, so that the foolishness of God might make them truly wise. In their wrestling with the paradoxical logic of God, they were forced to come to terms with the *Logos*, the mystery of God in Christ. Where finite and fallen human logic collides with the divine Word, Dietrich Bonhoeffer asserted, "Christ is the Counter-Logos. Classification is no longer a possibility, because the existence of this Logos spells the end of the human logos."[3] Bonhoeffer's point is not that human logic is eradicated or extinguished in its encounter with, and transformation by, God. His point is that all human strivings after the truth—which seek to speak before, around, and over the truth of God—do not allow the divine *Logos* to determine the shape and meaning of human logic. Our logic comes to an end, *and therefore a truly new beginning*, when it is transformed in Christ. This transformation is evident in the writings of the apostles, whose assumptions about reality were consistently shattered and re-formed in the presence of the Word become flesh. He took their preconceptions and conformed them to the truth of God. The apostles did not construct truth; the truth was *revealed* to them as the mystery of God. That mystery, as the apostle Paul makes clear, is not a mere concept, notion, or idea. The mystery of God is none other than Jesus Christ himself, the wisdom and knowledge of God. Christian theology has ever after been an annunciation of the great mystery (Greek, *mysterion*), whose name is Jesus Christ (Col. 2:2–3).

In order to apprehend the significance of mystery and its paradoxical entailments, and in order to forestall the objection that such terms invite irrational flights of fancy into the absurd, several points deserve clarification. First, theology necessitates and embraces mystery for the same reason that theology necessitates and embraces revelation: the triune God of Holy Scripture is disclosed and defined by the

---

3. Dietrich Bonhoeffer, *Christ the Center*, trans. Edwin H. Robertson (New York: Harper & Row, 1978), 30.

mystery of Christ. Mystery is not what occupies the void that exists where human reason has yet to determine the truth; mystery is the form that revelation and reality take in the person of our incarnate Savior. The apostle Paul employs the Greek term *mysterion* twenty-one times in his letters, with a wide range of meaning.[4] Most important for our purposes is that Paul refers to Jesus Christ *himself* as "God's mystery, . . . in whom are hidden all the treasures of wisdom and knowledge" (Col. 2:2–3). Christ simply is the mystery of God, the revelation of the redemptive purpose of God. The apostle elsewhere refers to this mystery as the indwelling of Christ in the saints (Col. 1:27), as the will of God to unite all things in heaven and on earth in Christ (Eph. 1:9–10), as the union of Jews and Gentiles in Christ's body (Eph. 3:4–7), and thus as the very substance of gospel proclamation (Rom. 16:25; Eph. 6:19; Col. 4:3). As Peter O'Brien notes, though there are various applications of the term *mysterion* in the Pauline corpus, "Christ is the starting point for a true understanding of the notion of 'mystery' in [Ephesians], as elsewhere in Paul."[5] Theology embraces mystery because theology embraces Christ as the transcendent revelation of God's purpose in creation and redemption. Christ illumines human understanding, not in spite of the fact that he is the mystery of God, but precisely because he is that mystery. Put forthrightly: the revelation of the Word of God does not eradicate mystery—the revelation *is* the mystery, and the mystery is Jesus.[6]

---

4. Marcus Peter Johnson, *One with Christ: An Evangelical Theology of Salvation* (Wheaton: Crossway, 2013), 193.

5. Peter T. O'Brien, "Mystery," in *The Dictionary of Paul and His Letters*, ed. Gerald F. Hawthorne, Ralph P. Martin, and Daniel G. Reid (Downers Grove, IL: IVP Academic, 1993), 623.

6. Michael Reeves instructively notes: "God *is* a mystery, but not in the alien abductions, things-that-go-bump-in-the-night sense. . . . God is a mystery in that who he is and what he is like are secrets, things we would never have worked out by ourselves. But this triune God has revealed himself to us. Thus the Trinity is not some piece of inexplicable apparent nonsense. . . . To know the Trinity is to know God, an eternal and personal God of infinite beauty, interest and fascination. The Trinity is a God we *can* know, and forever grow to know better." *Delighting in the Trinity: An Introduction to the Christian Faith* (Downers Grove, IL: IVP Academic, 2012), 12 (emphasis original).

A second point of clarity involves the relationship between mystery and paradox. If revelation assumes mystery, then mystery entails paradox. If mystery is the substance of revelation, then paradox is its shape. Because God's self-disclosure *transcends* our finite capacities, that self-disclosure inevitably invites us into realities that do not admit of solution or explanation. Encountered by the Word of God, we come face-to-face with a mystery that calls us to confess truths which, on their face, appear contrary to natural human cognition. Christian theology acknowledges this appearance to the contrary with the postulate of paradox, an acceptance that two seemingly contradictory truths can both be entirely true. Christian theology steps humbly into this tension created by God's invasion of our assumptions about truth and reality. Fleming Rutledge perceptively captures the importance of paradox for Christian theology: "Christian theology and the Christian life are best found on the frontiers, where our thinking and doing are engaged by the dynamic tension between two seemingly contradictory truths. At all times, our tendency to want to smooth over this tension is undercut by the self-correcting confession of the apostle when he declared, 'I decided to know nothing among you except Jesus Christ and him crucified'" (1 Cor. 2:2).[7] Theology involves the postulate of paradox because this postulate serves to clarify, not needlessly and endlessly obscure, the mystery that we encounter in Jesus Christ. "Paradox," writes Roger Hazelton, "has its own tactical role to play in the reflective discourse of faith. Its purpose is not to mystify but to clarify, yet in such a way that it is mystery which is made clear."[8] Like mystery, paradox is not the attribution of what cannot be truly known by human reason. Paradox, rather, is the way that Christians allow the mystery of Christ to shape our reason in accordance with that mystery. In other words, mystery assumes a paradoxical form precisely because the substance

7. Fleming Rutledge, *The Crucifixion: Understanding the Death of Jesus Christ* (Grand Rapids: Eerdmans, 2015), 33.

8. Roger Hazelton, "The Nature of Christian Paradox," *Theology Today* 6, no. 3 (October 1949): 331.

of paradox is mystery. For that reason, the affirmation of paradox is a welcome inevitability in all genuinely Christian theology:

> It is plain that when a Christian tries to say what creation, sin, or redemption mean he lands inevitably in some sort of paradox or other. When he explains how the universe is fashioned by God's will out of nothing, or how man's God-given freedom is his source of sin, or how death serves to illuminate life, he must express himself in a frankly paradoxical way, for he is himself engaged in a paradoxical task. How can man say what God is, or even what man is in the light of God? Clearly there is something in our faith which resists all tidy, neat, non-paradoxical formulas. The entire history of Christian theology bears witness and none can honestly deny it.[9]

Hazelton may well have gone on: when a Christian tries to say how a virgin can give birth, how Jesus can be both fully God and fully human, and how a man once dead can be alive, there too the Christian is no less constrained by the postulate of paradox. Paradox is a necessary aspect of theological confession because, as John Calvin asserted, "everything that is announced concerning Christ seems very paradoxical to human judgment."[10] Postulating paradox, therefore, allows the Christian to rationally express the mystery of Christ in a way that admits its uniquely authoritative form of reason.

A third and final point of clarity is apologetic: How can theology defend itself against the charge that it trades in rational contradictions and logical absurdities? The answer is that paradox and mystery are of a different species than contradiction. A paradox expresses two entirely true assertions at the same time, while a contradiction involves the assertion of two truths that are impossible to hold

---

9. Hazelton, "Nature of Christian Paradox," 326. Kallistos Ware observes: "We see that it is not the task of Christianity to provide easy answers to every question, but to make us progressively aware of a mystery." *The Orthodox Way*, 16.

10. John Calvin, *Calvin's Commentaries*, Calvin Translation Society (Edinburgh, 1844–56; reprinted in 22 vols., Grand Rapids: Baker Books, 2003), 19/2:218, on Rom. 6:1.

together at the same time. It is therefore, according to the Christian, no contradiction at all to assert that Jesus is fully God and fully man, or that Jesus has been crucified and is now alive. These are not contradictions but two simultaneously true facts. A contradiction, to be clear, would necessitate an assertion that Jesus is God and *not* God, or that Jesus is both dead *and* alive—the equivalent of a square circle. These are plainly contradictions, and Christian theology rejects them. Having said that, Christians must never begin to think they can allay each and every suspicion about our supposed logical inconsistencies—paradoxes will always strike some as illogical. But we must insist that we do not seek after or embrace nonsense. The postulate of paradox does not obscure human reason; it illumes it. Mystery does not abdicate reality; it affirms it.

Divine revelation entails and assumes mystery and paradox for the simple reason that God is never One we might have predicated or imagined. The revelation of God is new, strange, and unexpected. We need look no further than the prophets and apostles who, in their various encounters with God, were frequently stunned, bewildered, and even incredulous about who God is and what he does. They were compelled to submit their notions about divine being and acting to the reality that only God is capable of defining. The human authors of Holy Scripture were made to reckon with a God who would not be constrained by their religious or rational preconceptions. They were forced, in other words, to reckon with the mystery of God. When they came face-to-face with the sheer God-ness of God, they encountered One who can be truly known and utterly trusted—and above all delighted in. And yet this God could never be tamed or managed, domesticated or deconstructed.

The holy discernment needed to understand and rejoice in the gospel necessitates an acknowledgment of the gospel's paradoxical nature—the occasion for awe, wonder, and worship. It is also, as Hans Boersma notes, the occasion for rational modesty: "The modesty that theology needs is the recognition that we cannot rationally comprehend God. Theology is based on mystery and enters into mystery.

. . . Modern theology's problem is its rational confidence—and thus, ultimately, its pride."[11] For several centuries, Christians have been inordinately enchanted with what amounts to a dangerous liaison with the logical methodologies, and apparent certitudes, of Enlightenment rationalism, which are generally suspicious of mystery and paradox. Modern theology is too often tempted by a type of logic that ultimately undermines faith, reason, and worship. The church must be called, time and again, to confess and believe that our understanding of God and reality is by no means obscured and diminished but rather illumined and enriched by an affirmation of mystery.[12]

When the church embraces the mysterious and paradoxical nature of her faith and worship, she does so not out of irrationality or ignorance but because the church is called into the very deepest logic and reason of both God and man. To accept mystery and paradox keeps us both perfectly rational and perfectly sane. What G. K. Chesterton applies to the "ordinary man" applies all the more to the regenerate one:

> Mysticism keeps men sane. As long as you have mystery you have health; when you destroy mystery you create morbidity. The ordinary man has always been sane because the ordinary man has always been a mystic. He has permitted the twilight. . . . He has always cared more for truth than for consistency. If he saw two truths that seemed to con-

---

11. Hans Boersma, *Heavenly Participation: The Weaving of a Sacramental Tapestry* (Grand Rapids: Eerdmans, 2011), 26–27.

12. Alexander Schmemann contends: "Theology as proper words and knowledge *about* God is the result of the knowledge *of* God—and in Him of all reality. The 'original sin' of post-patristic theology consists therefore in the reduction of the concept of knowledge to rational or discursive knowledge or, in other terms, in the separation of knowledge from 'mysterion.'" *For the Life of the World: Sacraments and Orthodoxy*, 2nd ed. (Crestwood, NY: St. Vladimir's Seminary Press, 2002), 141 (emphasis original). Because the proper preoccupation of theology is the living God, knowledge *about* God is, in itself, entirely insufficient. To truly know God is to know him in keeping with who he actually is: a personal being rather than a fact, idea, or concept. The difference between knowing about God and knowing God is not unlike the difference between knowing about one's spouse and knowing one's spouse. The difference makes all the difference!

tradict each other, he would take the two truths and the contradiction along with them. His spiritual sight is stereoscopic, like his physical sight: he sees two different pictures at once and yet sees all the better for that. . . . The morbid logician seeks to make everything lucid, and succeeds in making everything mysterious. The mystic allows one thing to be mysterious, and everything else becomes lucid. . . . The cross, though it has at its heart a collision and a contradiction, can extend its four arms forever without altering its shape. Because it has a paradox in its centre it can grow without changing.[13]

Rejoicing in the Foolishness of God

Chesterton's collision and contradiction refer, of course, to the paradox of the crucified Christ. This paradox is the ground and substance of all subsequent Christian proclamation and, indeed, the very center of the church's joy, assurance, and conviction. Paul refers to the paradox of our crucified Savior as a "stumbling block" (Greek, *skandalon*) to the Jew and "foolishness" to the Gentile. Here is a paradox that scandalizes the world—Jew and Gentile alike—but in which the church rejoices. The paradox is that Jesus is both victim and victor, that Jesus bore our sin to bury it forever, that Jesus put death to death by death, that Jesus is the Savior of sinners who slayed him. Chesterton is right: if we allow one thing to be mysterious, "everything else becomes lucid." Jesus Christ is the light of the world. He banishes darkness and illumines all things, without ever surrendering his inscrutability. Trained in the gospel of our crucified Lord, the church is called to become theologically wise—truly logical, rational, discerning, and clear-sighted—to bow before the great paradox, the foolish wisdom of God:

> Where is the one who is wise? Where is the scribe? Where is the debater of this age? Has not God made foolish the wisdom of the world? For since, in the wisdom of God, the world did not know God through wisdom, it pleased God through the folly of what we preach to save

13. G. K. Chesterton, *Orthodoxy* (Colorado Springs: Shaw, 2001), 31–33.

those who believe. For Jews demand signs and Greeks seek wisdom,
but we preach Christ crucified, a stumbling block to Jews and folly to
Gentiles, but to those who are called, both Jews and Greeks, Christ
the power of God and the wisdom of God. For the foolishness of God
is wiser than men, and the weakness of God is stronger than men.
(1 Cor. 1:20–25)

The cross is central to any authentic Christian theology, but the
church's embrace of divine foolishness neither begins nor ends at
Golgotha. The divine mysteries, after all, are myriad. They constitute
the basis of every last article of the Christian faith. To name but a
few: Christians readily and heartily affirm that God is three persons,
yet one personal being; that God created all things, yet from no thing;
that in the incarnation the Creator became a creature without ceasing
to be Creator; that Jesus Christ is both fully God and fully human;
that a virgin gave birth; that One once dead now lives forevermore.
It is as unnecessary as it is futile to deny the inevitability of paradox
in Christian thought. If we sacrifice the paradox, we lose the mystery.
And if we lose the mystery, we forfeit the glorious truth of God's
being and action on behalf of humankind.

The mysteries at the heart of biblical revelation and at the center
of Christian faith compel the church to confess and adore them, allowing them to shape our understanding of reality. The historic creeds
of Christianity are exemplary instances of the church's holy desire to
enshrine our mysterious faith. Once we expurgate ourselves from the
erroneous notion that the creeds are philosophically derived attempts
to intellectualize Christian doctrine, we can affirm with Grounds
that what we possess in these formularies are doctrinal elaborations
of the mysteries of the gospel and the gospel's God. "For at bottom
what are those creeds except distilled paradoxes?"[14] There is a common misconception that the early church, attempting to accommo-
date the strictures and pressures of Hellenic thought, borrowed from
Greek philosophy to render the gospel suitably rational. Wherever

14. Grounds, "Postulate of Paradox," 6.

this erroneous assumption has gained traction, it has damaged the church's witness and worship, suggesting not only that the church "solved" the great mystery of revelation but in fact that philosophy exchanged its place as handmaiden to theology and instead become its lord. It bears repeating, "What could be more un-Hellenic than the statement of the Creed that God 'was made man'!"[15] The Apostles' Creed, the Nicene Creed, the Athanasian Creed, the Chalcedonian Definition—all great formularies of Christian theology—do not attempt to *solve* anything. In truth, they are articulations of the *mysteries* that undergird the life, worship, and witness of the church. Each and every Sunday, the church rises and confesses in unison that God is one being in three persons; that God is the maker of heaven and earth; that Jesus was conceived by the Holy Spirit and born of the virgin Mary; that Jesus is *homoousion* with the Father; that he rose from the dead and ascended into heaven; and that the Holy Spirit is the Lord and Life Giver. This joyful confession is not an expression projected or deduced from the powers of our religious imagination or intellectual prowess. We are giving expression to mysteries that originate from the miracle of divine revelation. These mysteries are received, not constructed. We do not define them; they define us.

The mysteries of the Christian faith are deeply embedded in the church's weekly worship, where we are taught to stand and confess realities that lie beyond our comprehension. The Book of Common Prayer, for example, is entirely typical when it calls the people of God to praise God as follows: "Therefore we proclaim the *mystery of faith*: Christ has died. Christ is risen. Christ will come again."[16] This liturgical commonplace, found throughout the millennia of Christian worship, is an unabashed acknowledgment that the central truths of the gospel—Jesus's death, resurrection, and second coming—are true

---

15. James B. Torrance, "The Vicarious Humanity of Christ," in *The Incarnation: Ecumenical Studies in the Nicene-Constantinopolitan Creed A.D. 381*, ed. Thomas F. Torrance (Eugene, OR: Wipf & Stock, 1998), 132.

16. *The Book of Common Prayer* (New York: Oxford University Press, 1979), 363 (emphasis added).

because they are mysteries and mysteries because they are true. Unlike solutions or explanations, which are singularly ill-disposed to invite adoration, mysteries invite us to the kind of awe-filled delight that brings us out of ourselves and into transcendent realities that sustain our lives in the Truth. A proper understanding of mystery, therefore, dispels two theological myths regnant in the contemporary church: first, that it is more fruitful to the minds and hearts of the faithful to pursue rational explanations of divine mysteries than to bow before them in humble submission; and second, that humble submission to mystery constitutes an escape into irrationality, a callous and perhaps careless trespass against fixed assumptions about what is "true" or "logical." Chesterton's quip—"The riddles of God are more satisfying than the solutions of man"—may be taken as sufficient to dispel either myth.[17] The mystery of God is ultimately satisfying because it is essentially rational, and ultimately rational because it is essentially satisfying. And we become amenable to logic only as we are conformed to the mystery of the *Logos*. One can sense the satisfaction kindled from God's riddled and foolish logic in Augustine's poetic musings on the great mystery of our Lord's incarnation:

> The Maker of man became Man that He, Ruler of the stars, might be nourished at the breast; that He, the Bread, might be hungry; that He, the Fountain, might thirst; that He, the Light, might sleep; that He, the Way, might be wearied by the journey; that He, the Truth, might be accused by false witnesses; that He, the Judge of the living and the dead, might be brought to trial by a mortal judge; that He, Justice, might be condemned by the unjust; that He, Discipline, might be scourged with whips; . . . that He, the Foundation, might be suspended upon a cross; that Courage might be weakened; that Security might be wounded; that Life might die.[18]

17. G. K. Chesterton, introduction to *The Book of Job* (London: Cecil Palmer & Hayward, 1916), xxii.

18. Augustine, *Sermons on the Liturgical Seasons*, trans. Sister Mary Sarah Muldowney, vol. 38 of *The Fathers of the Church*, ed. Roy Joseph Deferrari (New York: Fathers of the Church, 1959), 28.

In each phrase the apparent contradiction is obvious, yet truer words have scarcely been written. As Augustine demonstrates so beautifully, mystery and paradox are not enemies of reason; they are the basis and redemption of reason.

The Triumph of Mystery

"Divine Mystery," Katherine Sonderegger writes, "is not a sign of our *failure* in knowledge, but rather our *success*. It is because we *know* truly and properly—because we obey in faith the First Commandment—that God is mystery."[19] The time has come again for us as Christians to set aside sophomoric notions that the affirmation of mystery is a concession to irrationality. Such notions are oblivious to the fact that divine revelation bestows what is otherwise unavailable to us. Indeed, the very fact that we believe in God, as Sonderegger points out, is a product not of self-generated discovery but of obedience to the mystery of God's revelation. This obedience anchors the church in the truth, sheltering her from the temptation of that most deadly of sins: pride. The vice of unbridled curiosity, which Michael Allen calls the "noetic manifestation of pride," tempts us to pursue the task of *description* or *solution* when we ought to cultivate the virtue of *dependence*.[20] It is dependence, a near synonym for faith, that leads us to apprehend (not comprehend) the reality that grounds all logic and reason.

When we erroneously set faith against reason, we advance a titanic misunderstanding about the true nature of both faith *and* reason.

---

19. Katherine Sonderegger, *Systematic Theology*, vol. 1, *The Doctrine of God* (Minneapolis: Fortress, 2015), 24 (emphasis original). For this reference we are indebted to Michael Allen's excellent essay "The Knowledge of God," in *Christian Dogmatics: Reformed Theology for the Church Catholic* (Grand Rapids: Baker Academic, 2016), 12. Allen goes on to quote Karl Barth: "[God] remains a mystery to us *because* He Himself has made Himself so clear and certain to us." *Church Dogmatics* II/1, ed. G. W. Bromiley and T. F. Torrance, trans. T. H. L. Parker et al. (Edinburgh: T&T Clark, 1957), 3 (emphasis Allen).

20. Allen, "Knowledge of God," 13.

Shipwrecked on a false dichotomy, we begin to view faith and reason as foes rather than friends, as enemies rather than allies. Typically, this results in an attempt to reason our way *to* faith, a false and futile start if ever there was one. Though faith and reason are indeed allies, the relationship is not codependent. There is good reason why *sola fide* is a constitutional feature of Protestant theology but *sola ratione* is not. We apprehend Jesus by "faith alone," not by "reason alone." And it is Jesus alone who sets our reason to rights, justifying our intellect. It is always faith before reason, and therefore reason because of faith; the result is faithful reason. The relationship between the mystery of faith and the pursuit of reason has been nearly canonized by the dictum of St. Anselm, archbishop of Canterbury (1033–1109): "I do not seek to understand so that I may believe, but I believe so that I may understand; and what is more, I believe that unless I do believe I shall not understand."[21] Faith seeking understanding indicates the order in which the church engages reality: faith before reason, *Logos* before logic, foolishness before wisdom. The "before" is all-important. Yet while we insist that faith precedes reason, faith does not bear reason begrudgingly; rather, faith bears reason with open arms, in that faith is the womb of true reason. Faith is never the substitute nor the despair of reason but the highest and holiest form of it.

Anselm's adage has not proved nearly so controversial as that of his predecessor in the faith, the early church father Tertullian (155–240), who is commonly thought to have coined the phrase "*Credo quia absurdum*" ("I believe because it is absurd"). This is an ultimately erroneous attribution that has generated much more heat than light, not only among Christians but also among their cultured detractors. Yet the fact that Tertullian never technically uttered this phrase should not blind us to the fact that his actual claim is no less provocative. *Credo quia absurdum* is a loose paraphrase of this: "The Son of God was crucified; I am not ashamed because men must needs be ashamed *of*

---

21. Anselm, *Proslogion*, in *The Prayers and Meditations of Saint Anselm with the "Proslogion,"* trans. Benedicta Ward (New York: Penguin, 1973), 244.

it. And the Son of God died; it is by all means to be believed, because it is absurd [*ineptum*]. And He was buried, and rose again; the fact is certain, because it is impossible [*quia impossibile*]."[22] This passage makes it obvious enough that Tertullian was not hunting for outlandish oddities on which to ground faith. He is neither an antirationalist nor a rationalist. He is doing something altogether more biblically faithful: he is acknowledging that the crucifixion, death, and resurrection of God the Son *transcend and reorder* the bounds of rational thought. After all, if Jesus is able to fit neatly and comfortably within our preconceived notions of reality, we have every reason to wonder whether he is just another mythological projection of our religious sensibilities—a self-generated phantom we arbitrarily decided to deify and glorify.[23] The entirely paradoxical and mysterious nature of our Lord's person and work defies all presumptive, reasonable expectations. Tertullian's unvarnished admission of this puts him in the excellent company of prophets and apostles alike, whose presuppositions about God were consistently challenged and overturned by the strange and unanticipated way in which he reveals himself. So the concerted efforts to defend Tertullian from the charge of irrationality say much more about us than they do about him. Tertullian, after all, affirms no more and no less than the apostle Paul regarding the unfathomable enigma of Christ's cross and empty tomb. For Paul it is "foolishness" and for Tertullian it is "absurd." The difference is negligible.[24]

Theology is at its best when it recognizes itself in service of a mysterious Master. Indeed, when theology is free from preconceived

---

22. Tertullian, *On the Flesh of Christ*, in *ANF*, 3:525 (emphasis original).

23. Among the great ironies of the peculiarly modern fascination with rationally defending Jesus is that he nearly always becomes superfluous in the process: a Jesus who is not mysterious is not worth knowing or worshiping. We need look no further for an illustration than the secularization of the West.

24. John Webster contends: "The charge of 'foolishness' is a permanent accompaniment for any authentically Christian theology which is serious about struggling against sin in the intellectual realm: the reproach identifies that the question of the regeneration of the mind can never be laid aside in the way in which theology responds to its critics." "Incarnation," in *The Blackwell Companion to Modern Theology*, ed. Gareth Jones (Oxford: Blackwell, 2004), 9.

criteria about what constitutes reality, it is free to confess the truth. "Christian theology," notes John Behr, "is specifically a witness to the transforming power of God revealed in the Passion of Christ . . . and invites all to see reality in him." Theology, Behr continues, "is the confession of the truth, Christ himself, who does not stand subject to any criterion other than himself, the Lord of all creation and its history."[25] The question for the church should never be whether faith is reasonable, as if that question might be decided on the basis of a rationality independent of its Creator and Redeemer. A rationality that seeks to confer lordship on Christ—only after he has servilely met its demands—is an oxymoron of the first order, because conferred lordship is a self-evident expression of *actual* absurdity. The real question for the church is whether our faith is in accordance with the Truth, the *Logos*. It is this second question, the real question, which leads the church into a mortification of vivification of its intellectual existence. The crucified and resurrected Christian mind happily accepts that we have entered a reality not of our own making. The reality of God will always be wonderful and arresting; but it will always be true. The church is therefore under a holy constraint to resist the commonly held assumption that the so-called real world is a legitimate starting point for our encounter with divine revelation. Like golden crowns cast down before the golden sea, our conceptions of reality must be laid before the Lord, lest we begin to imagine that the revelation of God is yet another appendix to our knowledge that need only be justified in the court of "relevance." Robert Jenson highlights the danger when the church presumes reality rather than succumbing to it: "When the Bible lacks force in the church, it is regularly—from the time of the apostles to post-Christendom—because we presume that the 'real' world is some other world than the one that opens in the Bible, and that what we have to do is figure out how to make the Bible effective in the putatively 'real' world. The thing is: it cannot be

25. John Behr, *The Mystery of Christ: Life in Death* (Crestwood, NY: St. Vladimir's Seminary Press, 2006), 180–81.

done. The Bible is in fact ineffective and *irrelevant* in our so-called
'real' world, because the Bible does not acknowledge that our 'real'
world deserves the adjective."[26] Because reality is defined by God,
theology must hold in abeyance all of its prideful conceptions about
the ostensibly "real" world, instead opening its heart and mind to
a strange and new world that is both like and unlike the world with
which we have become familiar. "A world opens [in the Bible] that is at
first our earth, and then is strange and new beyond our conceptions,
and then again with all its novelty and discontinuity is somehow the
world we truly inhabit."[27]

If we may slightly rephrase Jenson's point: Christian thought does
not cease to exist in accordance with the way God originally created
reason to function. Nevertheless, because of the fall of humanity into
sin, theology must undergo the mysterious and paradoxical newness
of Christ in order to be truthful, faithful, and logical. Christ is the
New Creation, not because he jettisons the original creation but
because he enters it to fashion it anew. Our access to this new reality
requires not an obliteration of the old but its transformation through
crucifixion and resurrection. The embrace of mystery is the church's
way of acknowledging that God has put to death all of our vain and
curious speculations about reason and logic so that he might give us
new and everlasting life in Christ. What is true for the salvation of
our souls is every bit as true for the salvation of our minds: *there is
no other way to life than through death.*

Again, let us be clear: theology's dependence on mystery and paradox is not an intellectual retreat into the unknown, a sophomoric silo

26. Robert W. Jenson, "The Strange New World of the Bible," in *Theology as
Revisionary Metaphysics: Essays on God and Creation*, ed. Stephen John Wright
(Eugene, OR: Cascade, 2014), 150 (emphasis original).
27. Jenson, "Strange New World of the Bible," 148. Richard John Neuhaus demonstrates the liturgical implications of Jenson's statement: "Yet it is precisely in liturgy
that, with exquisite lucidity, we come to terms with the thus and so-ness of everyday
experience. The real world is the world of which Christ is King. In signaling that
truth, the Church makes its most important and most distinctive contribution to the
here and now." *Freedom for Ministry*, rev. ed. (Grand Rapids: Eerdmans, 1992), 134.

for the rationally unsophisticated. Quite the opposite; theology demands *more* of the intellect, not less. The deepest and most profound access to reality is determined and defined by Jesus, who is himself the mystery of God. It is only in and through this mystery that we really and truly apprehend the depths of truth. It is worth quoting Blaise Pascal once more: "Not only do we only know God through Jesus Christ, but we only know ourselves through Jesus Christ; we only know life and death through Jesus Christ. Apart from Jesus Christ we cannot know the meaning of our life or our death, of God or of ourselves."[28] It would be altogether disingenuous to accuse Pascal of being irrational or illogical—he was a brilliant polymath, exceedingly competent as a mathematician, philosopher, and physicist. Still, he knew well that the deepest, most-fundamental realities of knowledge—of God and ourselves, of life and death—require knowledge of Christ.

Thomas F. Torrance reflects a wide-ranging testimony of Christian witness, from apostles to church fathers to Reformers, when he insists that God's revelation of reality in Jesus Christ is not a fact accessible to us apart from that revelation, not a datum that we may facilely assimilate into our previous modes of rationality: "We cannot compare the fact of Christ with other facts, nor can we deduce the fact of Christ from our knowledge of other facts. The fact of Christ comes breaking into the continuity of our human knowledge as an utterly distinctive and unique fact, which we cannot understand in terms of other facts, which we cannot reduce to what we already know. It is a new and unique fact without analogy anywhere in human experience or knowledge."[29] Jesus comes to us in a way that forces us to reconceive all that we previously felt self-confident assuming about reality, reorienting our minds and hearts to the One through and for whom all things in heaven and on earth were created. Apart from

28. Blaise Pascal, *Pensées*, trans. A. J. Krailsheimer (New York: Penguin, 1995), no. 417, p. 141.

29. Thomas F. Torrance, *Incarnation: The Person and Life of Christ*, ed. Robert T. Walker (Downers Grove, IL: IVP Academic, 2008), 1.

the mystery of Christ, we remain in bondage to thought-forms that *distance* us from reality. Joined to Christ, however, we are freed to know the truth of God, the world, and ourselves. As the eighteenth-century Scottish theologian Thomas Boston grasped, this is reason for exuberant confession and deep rejoicing: "The Gospel is a doctrine of mysteries. O what mysteries are here! The Head in heaven, the members on earth, yet really united! Christ in the believer, living in him, walking in him: and the believer dwelling in God, putting on the Lord Jesus, eating his flesh and drinking his blood! This makes the saints a mystery to the world, yea, a mystery to themselves."[30] Like Pascal before him and Torrance after, Boston was keen to appreciate that the mystery of Christ and his gospel provide the deepest, most satisfying and gratifying answers to life's questions. Theology thrives when it postulates paradox, for it is a sure sign that theology, and the church that it serves, has embraced the mystery of Christ. And as impossible as it may seem to be or believe, all those who belong to Christ "have the mind of Christ" (1 Cor. 2:16).

Jerusalem, Athens, and the "Devil's Whore"

When it comes to Christian theology, and the relationship between faith and reason that it inevitably entails, it is difficult to imagine a more paradigmatic and perhaps controversial question than that posed by Tertullian: "What indeed has Athens to do with Jerusalem?" Because Athens was known as the epicenter of Greek philosophers and Jerusalem as the city of prophets and apostles, Tertullian's commentary is striking:

> The same subject-matter is discussed over and over again by the heretics and the philosophers; the same arguments are involved. . . . Unhappy Aristotle! who invented for these men dialectics, the art of building up and pulling down; an art so evasive in its propositions, so

---

30. Thomas Boston, *Human Nature in Its Fourfold State* (1799; repr., Carlisle, PA: Banner of Truth, 1989), 257.

far-fetched in its conjectures, so harsh in its arguments, so productive of contentions. . . . What indeed has Athens to do with Jerusalem? . . . Our instruction comes from "the porch of Solomon," who had himself taught that "the Lord should be sought in simplicity of heart." Away with all attempts to produce a mottled Christianity of Stoic, Platonic, and dialectic composition! We want no curious disputation after possessing Christ Jesus, no inquisition after enjoying the gospel![31]

Tertullian was obviously no advocate for advancing Aristotelian and Platonic philosophy in the church. To his mind, the city of the philosophers and that of the prophets and apostles had little in common. And if Tertullian's comments about the role of philosophically derived reason seem strong, we must brace ourselves for the words attributed to Martin Luther: "Reason is the devil's whore." Attempts of apologists eager to rescue Luther from himself, to defend him against the incendiary nature of this remark, are legion. Luther, we are told, is simply up to his usual hyperbolic high jinks. We are reminded that his own life was marked by prodigious intellectual ability and output. Luther, we are assured, was neither a dullard nor a philistine. These mollifications are not entirely misguided, provided they do away with the caricatures that Luther's quip might invite—that is, with any suggestion that he was an enemy of reason per se. Yet these apologies can be premature and superficial when they do not take with

---

31. Tertullian, *Prescription against Heretics*, in *ANF*, 3:246. Echoing Tertullian, Andrew Purves and Charles Partee write: "The reality of God is the final problem for philosophy but the first certainty for theology." *Encountering God: Christian Faith in Turbulent Times* (Louisville: Westminster John Knox, 2000), 12. Moreover, Tertullian decries a "mottled Christianity" born of epistemological syncretism, to which Robert W. Jenson remarks: "We usually refer to the work of Greece's theologians with their own name for it, 'philosophy.' We have thereupon been led to think this must be a different *kind* of intellectual activity than theology, to which theology perhaps may appeal for foundational purposes or against which theology must perhaps defend itself. But this is a historical illusion; Greek philosophy was simply the theology of the historically particular Olympian-Parmenidean religion, later shared with the wider Mediterranean cultic world. . . . Theologians of Western Christianity must indeed converse with the philosophers, but only because and insofar as both are engaged in the *same* sort of enterprise." *Systematic Theology*, vol. 1, *The Triune God* (New York: Oxford University Press, 1997), 9–10 (emphasis original).

due seriousness Luther's consistent and insightful diatribe against the dangers of a rationality that does not bow before the mystery of divine revelation. So before we exonerate Luther by suggesting that he did not mean what he said, we ought to consider that he meant *exactly* what he said: reason can all too easily be employed in a way that denies and denatures its true place as a servant of the gospel, presuming instead that reason is the gospel's master. Luther had no patience for an exercise of reason that sauntered ahead of the gospel, dictating the terms on which the mysteries of that gospel were thereby determined—as if "reason" had some privileged status by which to act as judge and jury of divine revelation.

This understanding of reason prompted Luther to say, "As a young man must resist lust and an old man avarice, so reason is by nature a harmful whore. . . . Therefore, see to it that you hold reason in check and do not follow her beautiful cogitations. Throw dirt in her face and make her ugly. Don't you remember the mystery of the holy Trinity and the blood of Jesus Christ with which you have been washed of your sins? . . . Reason is and should be drowned in baptism."[32] Reason "drowned in baptism." There is the key! Like all other human faculties stained and stunted by sin, reason needs the purification of Christ's watery grave. Without that death which gives way to life, reason presumes to speak for God: "But the devil's bride, reason, the lovely whore comes in and wants to be wise, and what she says, she thinks, is the Holy Spirit. Who can be of any help then? Neither jurist, physician, nor king, nor emperor; for she is the foremost whore the devil has."[33] Unchecked and undrowned, reason needs a resounding rebuke. "'You cursed whore, shut up! Are you trying to seduce me into committing fornication with the devil?' That's the way reason is purged and made free through the Word of the Son of God."[34] Luther had no intent whatsoever of obliterating reason as a necessary aspect of Christian existence, but neither

32. Martin Luther, "The Last Sermon in Wittenberg, 1546," in *LW*, 51:376.
33. Luther, "Last Sermon in Wittenberg, 1546," 374.
34. Luther, "Last Sermon in Wittenberg, 1546," 376–77.

did he deem reason to be a neutral or dependable foundation for it. His inflammatory, often uncharitable, and, yes, offensive language is intended to make us not just reticent about but viscerally repulsed by intellectual idolatries that fool rather than fortify the church. In Christ, death always comes before life, and reason is certainly no exception to that rule. When, and only when, reason is drowned, purged, and resurrected, the devil's whore is transformed into the holy handmaiden of the Lord's bride.

If Luther's words prompt pause, it is because his strident opposition to unchecked reason represents a viewpoint largely forgotten by modern Christians.[35] Many of Luther's predecessors and successors shared his suspicion about a species of rationality that, in its attempt to provide a rationale for divine revelation, actually obscured and usurped it. Several centuries after Luther, and nearly two millennia after Tertullian, we observe Flannery O'Connor's far less inflammatory remark: "How incomprehensible God must *necessarily* be to be the God of heaven and earth. You can't fit the Almighty into your intellectual categories."[36] From Tertullian to Luther, from Anselm to O'Connor, from Calvin to Kierkegaard, from Athanasius to Pascal

---

35. Ronald N. Frost would have us remember: "Luther's greatest concern in his early reforming work was to rid the church of central Aristotelian assumptions that were transmitted through Thomistic theology. To the degree that Luther failed—measured by the modern appreciation for these Thomistic solutions in some Protestant circles—a primary thrust of the Reformation was stillborn. The continued use of Aristotle's works by Protestant universities during and after the Reformation promoted such a miscarriage. Despite claims to the contrary by modern proponents of an Aristotelian Christianity, Aristotle's works offered much more than a benign academic methodology. . . . Luther recognized that Aristotle's influence entered Christian thought through the philosopher's pervasive presence in the curricula of all European universities. In his scathing treatise of 1520, *To the Christian Nobility of the German Nation*, Luther . . . chided educators for creating an environment 'where little is taught of the Holy Scriptures and Christian faith, and where only the blind, heathen teacher Aristotle rules far more than Christ.'" "Aristotle's *Ethics*: The *Real* Reason for Luther's Reformation?," *Trinity Journal* 18, no. 2 (Fall 1997): 225.

36. Flannery O'Connor to Alfred Corn, May 30, 1962, in *The Habit of Being*, ed. Sally Fitzgerald (New York: Farrar, Straus and Giroux, 1979), 477. For this reference we are indebted to Brad S. Gregory, *The Unintended Reformation: How a Religious Revolution Secularized Society* (Cambridge: Harvard University Press, 2012), 31 (emphasis Gregory).

and Barth, many of the best and brightest Christian theologians register sanctified suspicion about unsanctified reason in the apprehension and articulation of divine revelation. Calvin's comment is indeed representative: "All theology, when separated from Christ, is not only vain and confused, but is also mad, deceitful, and spurious; for, though the philosophers sometimes utter excellent sayings, yet they have nothing but what is short-lived, and even mixed up with wicked and erroneous sentiments."[37] Here again we find not *dismissal* of the potential of philosophical reason but rather its *conditionality*; the excellent sayings of philosophers must be conditioned by the revelation of Christ and his unconditioned lordship. Without that condition the results are disastrous. Indeed, it is no exaggeration to say that the majority of the heresies that have plagued the church from her birth originate in philosophical attempts to offer well-meaning solutions to mysteries that do not need them. That is why most heresies tend to be of the christological and trinitarian type. Like heat-seeking missiles, heresies home in on the warm heartbeat of Christian confession. The most notorious of these—Arianism, Modalism, Apollinarianism, Nestorianism, Eutychianism, Gnosticism, and the like—all share at least one thing in common: they destroy the mysteries of Christ and the Trinity with varied attempts to solve them.[38]

The task of theology is not to offer explanations for and solutions to the transcendent self-disclosure of God in Christ Jesus. Rather, the task is to offer with equal measure of humility and confidence a faithful articulation of the mystery of God's revelation, the terms of which Christ alone determines. Theology must never forget, as Tom Smail reminds us, that "God is not an object available of human

---

37. John Calvin, *Calvin's Commentaries*, Calvin Translation Society (Edinburgh, 1844–56; reprinted in 22 vols., Grand Rapids: Baker Books, 2003), 18:85–86, on John 14:6.

38. Harold O. J. Brown observes: "Why is Christianity so productive of divisive opinions, held with great conviction, that lead to splits in the church and charges and countercharges of heresy? The reason is simple: Christianity consists of a message that claims to be absolutely true and that is at the same time deeply and perplexingly mysterious." *Heresies: Heresy and Orthodoxy in the History of the Church* (Peabody, MA: Hendrickson, 1988), 6.

investigation who can be intruded upon by human speculation; he is Lord both of his life and ours, and of our knowledge of him. If he is going to be known, it will be in a way of his own choosing and by a process of his own controlling."[39] When theology becomes enamored with merely human investigation, it devolves into self-styled speculation, the engine of error.

When the church loses her imagination—loses, that is, her fascination with divine mystery and paradox—she is vulnerable to wanderlust. Unsatisfied with revelation, in other words, the church is precariously positioned to be seduced by the sort of certitude and legitimacy that is governed by philosophical logic, the scientific method, and their own attending notions of noncontradiction. There is no reason to deny that these methodologies and criteria are indeed useful in their own right. But we must also not deny that the "proof" of divine revelation requires faith and obedience, not solution and explanation. Søren Kierkegaard saw the church's flirtation with the latter as a failure of love and nerve, a fearfulness and faintness of heart that signals a dangerous deficit in the impassioned commitment of faith: "For whose sake is the demonstration conducted? Faith does not need it, indeed, must even consider it its enemy. When faith, however, begins to feel ashamed of itself, when, like a young woman in love who is not satisfied with loving but subtly feels ashamed of the beloved and consequently must have it substantiated that he is something exceptional, that is, when faith begins to lose passion, that is, when faith begins to cease to be faith, then the demonstration is made necessary in order to enjoy general esteem from unbelief."[40] Proofs intended to demonstrate to the world that God *really does exist* only serve in the end to demonstrate that the question is somehow legitimate and, worse still, that the Lord's bride is so forlorn that even she believes

39. Tom Smail, *Like Father, Like Son: The Trinity Imaged in Our Humanity* (Grand Rapids: Eerdmans, 2006), 21.

40. Søren Kierkegaard, *Concluding Unscientific Postscript to "Philosophical Fragments,"* ed. Howard V. Hong and Edna H. Hong, Kierkegaard's Writings 12 (Princeton: Princeton University Press, 1992), 1:30–31.

such proofs are necessary. Kierkegaard's incisive and unsettling commentary is the context in which we can wonder whether "the most profound threat to Christian faith since the Enlightenment has not been the ridicule of the philosophes or the skepticism of Hume, but theistic proofs and Christians who know God exists."[41] When the church and her theologians become preoccupied with arguments about a god who is the conclusion of syllogisms and conjectures—a being not specifically Father, Son, and Spirit, but who might just as easily be Allah, Ra, or Zeus—it is an indication that Christians have become dispassionate and embarrassed, off message and off mission.

If the historic church has been characteristically reticent about a naked and unbridled rationalism and the dangers it poses to authentic Christian confession, it was never because theology rejects the faculty of human reason. After all, the intellect is basic to the image of God in the human being. The church is cautious, rather, because she knows that each and every divinely endowed capacity exercised by humanity requires the gift of redemption and re-creation in Christ Jesus. At her theological best, the church knows that knowledge of God, no less than any other aspect of human striving and desiring east of Eden, requires a mediator: "For there is one God, and there is one mediator between God and men, the man Christ Jesus" (1 Tim. 2:5). Theology is therefore happy to accept that Christ's mediatorial role extends to human reason, aware that without that mediation reason inevitably seeks to seize the role of mediator for itself. Theology is alive to the reality that Jesus Christ has plumbed the depths of our benighted intellectual arrogance to offer us new and unending intellectual life in himself. The unfathomable and never-ceasing blessedness of knowing our Lord Jesus in the mystery of his person and work, through which he grants us access to the life he shares with his Father in the

41. William Greenway, review of C. Stephen Evans's *Faith beyond Reason: A Kierkegaardian Account, Christian Century* (Sept. 2000): 924. Alister McGrath similarly notes: "The English experience suggested that nobody really doubted the existence of God until theologians tried to prove it." *The Twilight of Atheism: The Rise and Fall of Disbelief in the Modern World* (New York: Doubleday, 2006), 31.

communion of the Holy Spirit, is a knowledge that he describes as eternal life. This knowledge transcends and qualifies all others, is apprehended nowhere but in him, and is the content of and context for all holy theology. Alan Torrance is therefore exactly right: "Proper epistemic function vis-à-vis God must be interpreted in the light of an all-embracing conception of participation *en Christo*—that is, it is to be interpreted as the gift of participating by the Spirit in the incarnate Son's epistemic, noetic, and semantic communion with the Father."[42] Theology is a gift. It is a gift because it is an act of human reason that results from an encounter with the Lord Jesus, who, through sheer grace, allows us to participate in his knowing of the Father by the Holy Spirit. Theology is not an intellectual achievement, gained by rigorous attention to spiritual phenomena (religious studies). Theology is a *response*, a response to belonging to Christ, who opens our minds and hearts to the transcendence of our triune God, to mysteries we cannot solve, to paradoxes we cannot comprehend, to truth we cannot deny, and to a logic entirely conditioned by the *Logos*.

The church, we hasten to add, is not the only seeker of truth and meaning in this world. Cast into the epistemological abyss created by the fall, humans desperately seek to define reality for themselves and by themselves. If there is a recurrent and even insidious pattern in human strivings after the truth, it is that truth is imagined to be self-explanatory and subject to self-definition. And if ever there was an exemplary instance of such autonomous imagining, the US Supreme Court's majority decision in Planned Parenthood v. Casey (1992) certainly qualifies. Speaking for that majority, Justice Anthony Kennedy notoriously ventured this statement: "At the heart of liberty is the right to define one's own concept of existence, of meaning, of the universe, and of the mystery of human life."[43] Even if we acknowledge the breathtaking ignorance and arrogance of this remark, shall we not

42. Alan J. Torrance, "*Auditus Fidei*: Where and How Does God Speak?," in *Reason and the Reasons of Faith*, ed. Paul J. Griffiths and Reinhard Hütter (New York: T&T Clark, 2005), 51.
43. Planned Parenthood v. Casey, 505 US 833 (1992), paragraph 2.

be somewhat sympathetic? Kennedy, after all, is not so different from any other fallen descendant of our primal parents, beguiled and bested by a serpentine wisdom that turns us in on ourselves as we attempt to discern the mystery of truth, meaning, existence, and life: "Did God *actually* say?" (Gen. 3:1). Face-to-face with the wisdom of the world, theology must insist that nothing apart from the liberation we find in Christ can redeem us from the kind of myopic and solipsistic absurdities uttered by Justice Kennedy, or from their death-dealing consequences. It is Christ who teaches us to know and confess that true and everlasting human liberty consists in the God-given gift of having one's existence defined by his Son, our Lord Jesus, who in himself is the meaning of the universe and the mystery of all human life. In truth, it is impossible to escape the reality of mystery. The creation of the universe is a mystery; so too is the genesis of human life. Sin and evil are mysteries; so too are their counterparts misery and suffering. The incarnation of God the Son is a mystery; so too is the gospel of his death and resurrection. The union between Christ and his church is a mystery; so too are the sacraments that signal and fortify that union. The ascension of Christ to the right hand of God the Father is a mystery; so too is his coming again. These are mysteries one and all, precisely because they are revelations of the truth.

It is a colossal mistake to believe that theology involves the task of solving or explaining the reality of God or the world. Theology, on the contrary, is properly concerned with the mystery of God, whose incomprehensibility is the ground of all true comprehension. Theology is "devoted to the task of bringing all its statements into line with that great mystery, measuring its words by his Word, but forever in the confidence that he who ceaselessly judges our thought also patiently fulfills and consecrates it."[44] When it does so, when theology bends itself into conformity with the mystery of God revealed in the mystery of Christ, theology participates in the Truth of all truth, the *Logos* that defines all logic—the meaning and reality of God and of our world.

44. Hazelton, "Nature of Christian Paradox," 335.

6

Living Forward, Understanding Backward

The Eschatological Tension of Christian Theology

The church's liturgy helps us live theologically, rooting us in the one *Christ-reality*, so we can do the world the way it is meant to be done. Take, for example, the season of Advent, the four-week season in the liturgical calendar that leads up to Christmas Day. Advent derives its name from the Latin *adventus* (Greek, *parousia*), which means "coming," "arrival," or "presence." Fittingly, the beginning of Advent marks the beginning of each new liturgical year. For when the eternal Son of God became the newborn Son of Mary, when the Ancient of Days became but one day old, a new time entered and forever altered our world. So the message of Advent is, Wake up! Watch! Wait! It is a message of joyful anticipation for the Christ once wrapped in swaddling clothes to abide ever more fully in us and for the Christ now arrayed in searing splendor to come and judge the world in righteousness. Yes, the church observes the season of Advent as a time to prepare for Christmas *and* the second coming.[1] At the start of each new liturgical year the church is called to remember that our Christian existence is lived, and thus our theology is done, amid the eschatological tension of the now and not-yet. Indeed, as John Webster insists, "Christian faith is eschatological. It is a response to God's devastation of human life and history by the miracle of grace."[2] Our focus at present, then, is not on eschatological events, or even on the doctrine of eschatology per se, important as these are. Our focus is on the fact that theological formation takes place at the frontiers of eternity, on the edge of the age to come. For Christian theology, like the rest of our Christian existence, is conditioned by the new creation begun at Christ's *first* advent to be fully and finally realized at his *second* advent.[3]

The parousia, the coming and presence of Christ, is not solely out in front of us, disjointed from his first advent. Nor may our Lord's past and future comings be conflated into something monolithic. For the parousia is a multifaceted singularity that includes the birth, life, death, resurrection, ascension, and coming again of the mystery who is Immanuel, God with us.[4] From womb to tomb, the Christ who became what he created without ceasing to be Creator brought the reality of heaven to bear on earth, inaugurating a new creation amid the old. And in the ascension of our risen Lord, the reality of earth was brought to bear on heaven, as the firstfruits of the new creation were established and exalted at the right hand of the Father (1 Cor. 15:20–24; 2 Cor. 5:16–17; Eph. 1:10; Col. 1:20). Here is the

1. "Advent," in *The Oxford Dictionary of the Christian Church*, 3rd ed., ed. F. L. Cross and E. A. Livingstone (New York: Oxford University Press, 1997), 20–21.

2. John Webster, *The Culture of Theology*, ed. Ivor J. Davidson and Alden C. McCray (Grand Rapids: Baker Academic, 2019), 46.

3. Thomas F. Torrance, *Incarnation: The Person and Life of Christ*, ed. Robert T. Walker (Downers Grove, IL: IVP Academic, 2008), 313; Andrew Purves, "The Advent of Ministry: Torrance on Eschatology, the Church, and Ministry," in *Evangelical Calvinism*, vol. 2, *Dogmatics and Devotion*, ed. Myk Habets and Bobby Grow (Eugene, OR: Pickwick, 2017), 96–97.

4. G. C. Berkouwer, *The Return of Christ*, Studies in Dogmatics (Grand Rapids: Eerdmans, 1972), 140–41.

parousia that heals the breach between God and humanity, Creator and creation, heaven and earth, spirit and matter—affecting even time and space. It regulates the shape of the Christian life, the structure of human history, and the whole of the new creation now emerging as the old one passes away. The parousia in its future aspect, at Christ's second advent, shall therefore be in essential continuity with his first advent. For the coming of the Word made flesh is the material content of his coming again, as Christ's incarnate, earthly presence is fused with his ascended, heavenly presence in one indivisible parousia of the ages.[5] The angels thus prophesied at our Lord's ascension: "Men of Galilee, why do you stand looking into heaven? This Jesus, who was taken up from you into heaven, will come in the same way as you saw him go into heaven" (Acts 1:11). So we confess that "Jesus Christ is the same yesterday and today and forever" (Heb. 13:8), even as he proclaims, "I am the Alpha and the Omega, . . . who is and who was and who is to come, the Almighty" (Rev. 1:8).

Behold the majesty of Jesus Christ: his coming is of One now present, and his presence is of One yet to come. For it is the selfsame Christ to come who even now promises: "I am the vine; you are the branches. Whoever abides in me and I in him, he it is that bears much fruit, for apart from me you can do nothing" (John 15:5); "Where two or three are gathered in my name, there am I among them" (Matt. 18:20); "I am with you always, to the end of the age" (Matt. 28:20). If Christ were not now present with and in the church there could be no Christian existence, given that Christ's people have life not in themselves but in Christ, the head of the body. At the same time, if the Christ now present were not at once the Christ yet to come, we would have right here and now all that life in Christ can offer, making us a most pitiful lot (1 Cor. 15:19). Thanks be to God, the gift of the Eucharist assures us this is not the case. As often as we receive that sign and seal of our participation in Christ, that body-and-blood

---

5. Thomas F. Torrance, *Space, Time and Resurrection* (Grand Rapids: Eerdmans, 1976), 143–44.

promise of his life-giving presence, that tangible, tasteable testimony of the mystery that is Christ now in us, we "proclaim the Lord's death until he comes" (1 Cor. 11:26). This is why the Eucharist is not a feast that satiates our appetite, providing the sort of comfort that leaves us sluggish and sleepy, as if we were already at our destination. No, the Eucharist is a feast that whets our appetite and trains our palate for true food and true drink, providing the sort of comfort that steadies and strengthens us, so we may go forth into the world rejoicing in the power of the Spirit, awake and aware for the journey at hand.

Indeed, our Lord's now-and-coming presence is a paradox as instructive and illuminating as it is insoluble and inscrutable. Like all biblical paradoxes, it allows us to recognize reality in Christ, such that attempts to undo it do nothing but relegate us to nonreality. For the reality of Christ's now-and-coming presence permeates the truth of the gospel—that we now are and yet shall be resurrected in Christ, that we now are and yet shall be sanctified and glorified in Christ, that we now are and yet shall be redeemed and rendered new creations in Christ. To separate Christ's coming from his presence is thus to functionally, if not formally, reduce eschatology to some species of futurism or preterism (Latin, *praeter*; "past"). Futurism stresses Christ's second advent at the expense of duly recognizing his presence with and in his people now, undermining the reality of the church and the Christian life. And preterism stresses our present life in Christ at the expense of duly recognizing its future fulfillment, undermining the reality that the good work begun in us as the result of Christ's first advent shall be brought to completion only at his second advent (Phil. 1:6). But eschatology is neither futurism nor preterism, as its chief concern is the revelation, anticipation, and inaugurated realization of the future in the present.[6] In other words, Christian faith "is eschatological in the sense that it is a set of astonished human responses to the gospel of the new world. The gospel announces the unheard-of truth that sin and death have been set aside, that human

6. Donald G. Bloesch, *The Last Things: Resurrection, Judgment, Glory*, Christian Foundations (Downers Grove, IL: InterVarsity, 2004), 13.

life is caught up in the new creation, and that all are summoned to a life corresponding to the new thing which God has done."[7]

We are the Father's children now, and present partakers in God's triune glory, though what we shall be has not yet appeared (1 Pet. 5:1; 1 John 3:2). Raised to new and eternal life in Christ, we now have the firstfruits of the Spirit; yet we wait eagerly, longingly, groaning with the whole of creation for what is presently real to be utterly realized in the redemption of our bodies and the renewal of the cosmos (Rom. 8:19–25). Make no mistake: this eschatological tension of the now and not-yet is not a tension to balance, a paradox to resolve. Instead, it is a tension to inhabit and embrace, a paradox that brings other paradoxes in tow, all of which are meant to make us wholly present to the purposes of God in the present. Just as the church is crucial to the *where* of our theological formation, the now and not-yet is crucial to its *when*—the appointed time in the timing of God for us to mature in stature, to grow in every way toward the measure of Christ. Now we see truly yet dimly, but at Christ's appearing every last shadow shall succumb to light; now we know really yet partly, but then we shall know fully, even as we are fully known; now faith, hope, and love abide, and the greatest of these is love (1 Cor. 13:12–13).

Living Forward, Understanding Backward

Life can only be understood backward; but it must be lived forward.[8] This ranks among Søren Kierkegaard's most memorable pieces of proverbial wisdom, and for good reason. We are never any more human than on the day of our birth, though at that time we have but the slightest sense of self-awareness. What we understand about being human grows incrementally thereafter, and largely through lived experience. Similarly, husbands and wives are never any more married than on the

---

7. Webster, *Culture of Theology*, 63.
8. Søren Kierkegaard, *Kierkegaard's Journals and Notebooks*, vol. 11, part 1, *Loose Papers, 1830–1843*, ed. Niels Jørgen Cappelørn et al. (Princeton: Princeton University Press, 2019), IV.A.164.

day of their wedding. Yet five, ten, fifty years of living in one-flesh union grants them insight into marriage that they simply could not possess when they first exchanged marital vows. And we are never any more children of God than on the day of our new birth in Christ. Nonetheless, what it means to be a Christian is truly understood only by *being* a Christian. Kierkegaard's aphorism tells us something profound about life in general, and about the paradox of the Christian life in particular: committed entrance into this life is the condition not only for understanding it but also for understanding ourselves as transformed by it.

Accordingly, the first disciples are a study in living forward and understanding backward, as for some time they were puzzled and perplexed in Jesus's presence. "Can anything good come out of Nazareth?" demurred Nathanael at Jesus's lowly provenance (John 1:46). "Far be it from you, Lord! This shall never happen to you," scolded Peter, offended by Jesus's talk of his death and resurrection (Matt. 16:21–23). "You shall never wash my feet," contended the same disciple, again vexed by Jesus (John 13:8). "Lord, show us the Father, and it is enough for us," pleaded Philip, peering at the Son who perfectly images the Father (John 14:8). "Unless I see in his hands the mark of the nails, . . . I will never believe," insisted Thomas, incredulous in the wake of Jesus's ignominious death (John 20:24–25). "But we had hoped that he was the one to redeem Israel," grieved the two dejected disciples on route to Emmaus after Jesus's crucifixion, unaware that they were speaking with their resurrected Redeemer (Luke 24:21). Examples could be multiplied with ease, but the point is sufficiently clear. As the first disciples committed themselves to Jesus, he began to expose and overturn their misguided messianic expectations and assumptions. Indeed, as the full and final revelation of God, Jesus is the divine Truth who laid bare and pierced their hearts, transforming their minds and setting to rights their broken, distorted knowledge of God.[9] But despite being with Jesus for years, hearing his words

9. Kelly M. Kapic, "The Incarnation and Christian Existence: The Humiliation of the Name" (plenary address, Evangelical Theological Society, November 16, 2011, San Francisco), 2–3; Thomas F. Torrance, *The Mediation of Christ*, rev. ed.

and seeing his deeds, the disciples did not yet truly understand him. That occurred only after Jesus's crucifixion and exaltation, as they turned back to Scripture. Not to the Gospels and Epistles, of course, which were not yet written. Rather, the disciples turned back to what is now called the Old Testament and at last grasped what Jesus had told them: the Law, the Psalms, and the Prophets bear witness to him (Luke 24:25–27; John 5:39; cf. Acts 2:29–36; 18:28; 1 Pet. 1:10–12). Yes, the life of Israel, like the lives of the disciples, had to be lived forward yet understood backward.[10]

Let us be clear: the sort of understanding backward that the disciples undertook was *not* the historicizing approach of modernity. They did not situate Jesus squarely in the past and subject him to the judgment of historicist criteria. Nor did they turn back to the Old Testament as if it were a neutral narrative to be verified by impartial historiographers. For the disciples did not come to confess that Jesus is the Christ and God the Son simply by investigating reports about him, by traveling with him, or even by observing his marvelous and miraculous acts. Flesh and blood, says Jesus, did not reveal this to them (Matt. 16:17). The lesson here for our theological formation is all-important, and it is imperative that we learn it well. Our usual methods of human knowledge—historical inquiry, scientific analysis, philosophical reflection, and the like—clearly have much to commend. But these are inadequate when our desire is knowledge

---

(Colorado Springs: Helmers & Howard, 1992), 12. "It is commonplace in evangelical theology to tie the incarnation directly to Christ's reconciling and atoning death and resurrection—that is, to assert, rightly, that the Son of God took on our flesh in order to bear our sin on the cross and raise us to new life. But what is often overlooked is the corresponding reality that in joining himself to humanity, the Son came to reconcile and atone for—to crucify and resurrect—our broken and corrupted *knowledge* of God. The divide that Christ came to bridge between humanity and God includes the deep chasm in our hearts and minds between what we think we know about God and who God really is." John C. Clark and Marcus Peter Johnson, *The Incarnation of God: The Mystery of the Gospel as the Foundation of Evangelical Theology* (Wheaton: Crossway, 2015), 48 (emphasis original).

10. John Behr, *The Mystery of Christ: Life in Death* (Crestwood, NY: St. Vladimir's Seminary Press, 2006), 22.

of God, because God is not known by mere human perception, no matter how brilliant.[11] How an object is known must be determined by the nature of the object; and when that object is God, we must understand that he is uniquely Lord of his own self-disclosure in Jesus Christ. Thomas F. Torrance states the matter superbly:

> If Jesus Christ is really the Son of God then it must be clear that a quite different approach must be adopted toward understanding him from that required for any other figure in history—although even on a purely historical level, we cannot help but grant that we are confronted with something that is without parallel anywhere else in history. If . . . Jesus Christ stands before me as true man and true God, God who created this unity of man and God, then my whole knowing of him will be determined by his act, and will be made real and possible only through his act upon me. If God comes to me in Jesus Christ as my saviour then all my thought about Jesus Christ will take its rise from that act of salvation.[12]

With their thought taking rise from their crucified and exalted Savior, the disciples turned to the Hebrew Scriptures as to a theological thesaurus of language and imagery for entering deeper into the mystery of Christ. Indeed, the disciples came to understand that the Jesus they encountered in the breaking of the bread is the selfsame Christ anticipated in the Law, the Psalms, and the Prophets (Luke 24:25–27, 30–32). The New Testament, in turn, speaks not of a Christ relegated to the past and merely verified by the Hebrew Scriptures but of the Christ whose presence and action is interpreted by recourse to those Scriptures. The New Testament is a result neither of the apostles' novel musings about Jesus nor even of their extraordinarily insightful exegesis of the Old Testament. Their writings are the fruit of Israel's God opening his inner-triune life in the fullness of time through the revealing, reconciling acts of the Son and

11. Behr, *Mystery of Christ*, 16–17, 27.
12. Torrance, *Incarnation*, 13.

Spirit to shape human thought and speech into a vehicle capable of articulating a mystery that our usual methods of knowledge could never fathom. The witness of the apostles is the Father-ordained, Spirit-superintended testimony to the saving incursion and abiding presence of Jesus Christ in the church. And the Christ who reveals himself to us in the apostolic proclamation as the crucified and risen Lord in accordance with the Hebrew Scriptures (1 Cor. 15:3–4) is an eschatological figure, the coming One.[13]

The Ancient of Days has entered his glory, and he invites us to live forward, to live into the future with him, calling over his shoulder, as it were, like C. S. Lewis's Christ figure, Aslan the lion, "Come further in! Come further up!"[14] Living forward does not mean that our Lord is changing or evolving, developing or progressing. For he is always and ever exactly like himself, constant and consistent in his character, promises, and purposes. If Jesus Christ were not the same from age to age, world without end, we would be witless and reckless to entrust ourselves to him in body and soul, now and forever. And if he did not eclipse every measure except himself, subject to no standard but himself, he would not be uniquely or ultimately Lord of history, culture, and all creation. Neither, therefore, does living forward mean that we move beyond the faith once and for all delivered to the saints (Jude 3) or do anything but hold fast with heart and hands to the Christ once and for all revealed to the saints in Scripture. Living forward means that we embrace and inhabit the eschatological tension of the now and not-yet. It means that we resist the temptation to retreat from the challenges of discipleship to the bondage of complacency in our own Egypt. And it means that we relinquish any undue reliance on clarity regarding the path ahead, given that craving for clarity is a reticence to trust God masquerading as good sense—a cruel companion that fills and freezes us with fear. Theological formation is the result of our knowledge of God

13. Behr, *Mystery of Christ*, 17, 27.
14. C. S. Lewis, *The Last Battle*, Chronicles of Narnia 7 (New York: Harper Trophy, 1994), 197.

growing by degrees over time through the lived experience of trusting and obeying him amid the myriad seasons and situations of life; and because knowing God is the true substance, sweetness, and sum of our lives, we live forward, into the future, and into the ever-growing understanding that awaits us there.

Christians are described in Scripture as belonging to "the Way" (Acts 9:2; 19:23; 24:14, 22), which means that we are wayfarers, and that our theological formation is an enterprise in wayfaring. Jesus Christ is our guide on this journey, yet he is immensely more than just the One who knows the way to where we are going. He *is* the Way, himself our journey's path, purpose, and goal. So we are not settlers but sojourners (1 Pet. 2:11), called to walk in and with Christ by the lamp of Scripture and the Spirit who gives light even amid the palpable presence of darkness (Ps. 119:105; Gal. 5:16, 25; Eph. 5:8, 15; Col. 2:6–7; 1 John 1:6–7). Ours is thus an imperfect theology in progress, the theology of pilgrims (Latin, *theologia viatorum*); it is not the theology of the blessed (Latin, *theologia beatorum*), whose pilgrimage has ended, their goal attained in glory.[15] Kelly Kapic writes of this journey with the warmth and wisdom of one who has traveled it long and knows it well:

> Sometimes as theologians we find ourselves climbing sun-drenched mountains or descending into dark valleys; occasionally we are rewarded with an endless vista, while at other moments fog surrounds us and obscures our path. As with most long journeys, there will be times when we must stop to catch our breath, times when we may get lost and when we will do well to ask others for directions. Sometimes we take paths which do not take us where we expected, while at other times we turn a corner only to discover a wonderful view that we have been longing and struggling to reach.[16]

15. Kelly M. Kapic, *A Little Book for New Theologians: Why and How to Study Theology* (Downers Grove, IL: IVP Academic, 2012), 32–33; see the definition of "theology of the blessed" in Donald K. McKim, *The Westminster Dictionary of Theological Terms*, 2nd ed. (Louisville: Westminster John Knox, 2014), 319.

16. Kapic, *Little Book for New Theologians*, 33–34.

Pilgrim theology is theology for the eschatological tension of the now and not-yet, and it gives us tools to face reality—to think, feel, and say true things about the way things truly are. Free from the pretense that our theology is finished and flawless, devoid of any rough or ragged edges, we can be humble and teachable, unafraid of the vulnerability that theological formation requires. And free from the illusion that our goal is already attained, we can reject the facile triumphalism of overrealized eschatology, which acknowledges only the sunnier story line of the Christian life east of Eden and this side of glory. Life in the now and not-yet is both wonderful and horrible, magnificent and marred, breathtaking and heartbreaking—and to tell only one side or the other of this story is simply not to tell the truth. Pilgrim theology allows us to occupy this tension honestly, in gratitude and grief, with praise and lament, being of unfeigned good cheer, albeit sometimes through a vale of tears. It allows us in doubt to appeal, "I believe; help my unbelief!" (Mark 9:24). It allows us in confusion to confess, "Lord, to whom shall we go? You have the words of eternal life" (John 6:68). And it allows us to boast in the triune God of the gospel right in the teeth of the otherwise overwhelming specters of sin and death, not least our own. Pilgrim theology knows of whom it speaks, so while it is not finished or flawless, neither is it fickle or feckless, timid or tentative. Throughout this journey, we do not just traffic in truths; we are transformed by the incarnate Truth. All advances in our theological formation should thus be cherished as the choicest of treasures and held with tenacity against the host of headwinds we shall surely encounter until our wayfaring days at last reach their blessed end.

And our theological formation advances primarily as we grow in what have long been called the theological virtues: faith, hope, and love. Faith seeks and finds understanding, because faith is the obedience of our minds to the mystery of Christ, "the founder and perfecter of our faith" (Heb. 12:2). Here we must note that many moderns dichotomize faith and understanding, excluding faith from the sphere of knowledge. They assume that faith must either give way to knowledge or become operative when and where knowing ends. This is a secular notion of faith, but not at all a biblical one. Biblical faith is not antithetical to knowing, an alternative to knowing, or some superstitious vagary that falls short of knowing. Quite the contrary, the faith that binds us to Christ, "in whom are hidden all the treasures of wisdom and knowledge" (Col. 2:3), is the surest and highest form of knowing. In fact, Scripture tells us that faith is the assurance of what we hope for now but have not yet seen with our eyes, the grand and glorious gospel promises of God that are all "Yes!" in Christ (2 Cor. 1:20; Heb. 11:1). As such, Christian hope is neither the hope-for-hope's-sake optimism of glib positivity nor the hope-against-hope desperation of finger-crossing holdouts for lost causes. Christian hope is the firm and settled certainty that present realities shall indeed be fully realized, that what is truly ours in Christ right now shall be finally and radiantly manifest in the not-yet. All the while, the incarnate Love who first loved us calls forth a love in return that grants us a sort of second sight, the ability of faith and hope to know and understand now what has not yet come to full fruition. G. K. Chesterton is right: "Love is not blind; that is the last thing that it is. Love is bound; and the more it is bound the less it is blind."[17] So as we undertake the journey at hand, living forward and understanding backward all the while, let us pray like pilgrims with Anselm, "Lord, make me taste by love what I taste by knowledge; let me know by love what I know by understanding. . . . Draw me to you, Lord, in the fullness of love. I am wholly yours by creation; make me all yours, too, in love."[18]

Maturing into Childlikeness

The need of living forward to understand backward speaks volumes about how good and right it is for Christians to mature. This begins

17. G. K. Chesterton, *Orthodoxy* (Colorado Springs: Shaw, 2001), 101.
18. Anselm, "Meditation on Human Redemption," in *The Prayers and Meditations of Saint Anselm with the "Proslogion,"* trans. Benedicta Ward (New York: Penguin, 1973), 237.

at new birth, as those reborn in Christ are encouraged to long like insatiable infants for the pure spiritual milk of the gospel (1 Pet. 1:23–2:2). As grand as conversion is, however, it is the start of the Christian life, not its sum. Perpetual infancy, or even prolonged adolescence, is unnatural and abnormal at best. And when such a state is self-imposed, the result of sloth or negligence, it is positively sinful and shameful. For it is extravagance of the most wanton sort; the forfeiture of growing into the full stature and strength of the saints, and the abdication of being a teacher, shepherd, and parent in the faith to others. Milk alone—the bare basics of the Christian faith—is thus an inadequate long-term diet for Christian growth. It is not that we ever outgrow the basics; we most certainly do not. It is that the basics must be built on, supplemented and complemented with the stouter sustenance of solid food, the deep and bracing things of God that produce theological wisdom, fortitude, and resilience, that sharpen our ability to discern good from evil (1 Cor. 3:1–2; Heb. 5:11–14). These are the qualities that we sorely need to flourish in the eschatological tension of the now and not-yet. And this is the theological formation we require to set aside "childish ways" of thinking and speaking (1 Cor. 13:11; 14:20). We are to seek a maturity whose measure is Christ, "so that we may no longer be children, tossed to and fro by the waves and carried about by every wind of doctrine, by human cunning, by craftiness in deceitful schemes" (Eph. 4:14).

Scripture extols Christian maturity, often by contrasting that maturity with childishness. So it is all the more striking that Jesus extols children as emblematic of the kingdom, as those ahead of us, those we must emulate, and those to whose likeness we must aspire. Calling a child to himself, he punctuates this paradox: "Truly, I say to you, unless you turn and become like children, you will never enter the kingdom of heaven" (Matt. 18:3). We often assume that adulthood is the mark of maturation. But adulthood is never itself that mark, and if we are not careful, this misstep will take us far afield of it. Our Lord teaches that the maturation of which Scripture speaks is not from younger to older, from childhood to adulthood. No, his will is to see all of us, regardless of age, maturing into childlikeness. C. S. Lewis does not make the distinction between childish and childlike as we do here. Yet in this case the issue is purely semantic. Our meaning is the same, and Lewis makes a brilliant point:

> [Those] who treat "adult" as a term of approval, instead of as a merely descriptive term, cannot be adult themselves. To be concerned about being grown up, to admire the grown up because it is grown up, to blush at the suspicion of being childish; these things are the marks of childhood and adolescence. And in childhood and adolescence they are, in moderation, healthy symptoms. Young things ought to want to grow. But to carry on into middle life or even into early manhood this concern about being adult is a mark of really arrested development. . . . When I became a man I put away childish things, including the fear of childishness and the desire to be very grown up.[19]

Christian maturity does not make us more and more insistent on being grown up but less and less inhibited about being childlike in ways that are, in fact, Christlike. The measure of Christian maturity is Christ, who is by nature the only-begotten child of the Father and thus the epitome of true childlikeness. And while we have sinned and grown old, the Ancient of Days is younger than us.[20] What, therefore, does maturing into childlikeness mean for our theological formation? First and foremost, it means that our passion for truth and understanding should be marked by a passion for joy. For the fundamental fact of the Christian faith is the birth of the God-Word, our *Theos-Logos*, and that is "news of great joy" (Luke 2:10–11). And in the Upper Room Discourse, Jesus's richest and most robust theological teaching in the Gospels, he says, "These things I have spoken to you, that my joy may be in you, and that your joy may be full" (John 15:11). Indeed, Jesus promises on precisely the same occasion that in this world we will have tribulation (John 16:33). But our call is not to be sullen and surly in

19. C. S. Lewis, "On Three Ways of Writing for Children," in *Of Other Worlds: Essays and Stories* (New York: Harcourt Brace, 1966), 25.

20. Chesterton, *Orthodoxy*, 84.

the now, shuffling drearily toward the not-yet. To share in the mind of Christ is to share in the joy of Christ, and we dare not foster passion for the former but not the latter. Dorothy Sayers's quip is worth heeding: "The worst sin—perhaps the only sin—passion can commit, is to be joyless."[21] This is not a sin to which children are prone. Their abounding vitality is quick to express itself in rapturous joy, an instinctive ease of entering into joy, and a delightful self-forgetfulness that allows unabashed adoration and affection, all without the cynicism and self-conscious restraint that often plagues so-called grown-ups. Like the mind of Christ, the joy of Christ is known only by entering into it and being transformed by it. So one telltale sign that we are maturing into childlikeness will be our doing theology with more and more of the exuberance and anticipation that we would hope to find in a seven-year-old on Christmas morning.

Theological formation of this sort increases our capacity to enter with awe the wonder of God and the wellspring of Christ's joy: the triune life of love he shares with the Father in the fellowship of the Spirit. The Father gives all he has to the Son, and the Son seeks all he has in the Father, such that in childlike trust and love for the Father, the Son wills not to speak, act, or know independently of the Father (John 5:19–20, 30; 7:16–18; 12:49–50). Those all too concerned with being grown-ups find Christ's childlike deference to the Father blush-worthy. For it exposes a temptation as old as Eden: to know on one's own terms for one's own ends, to believe that knowledge itself is power, and to seek self-satisfied pleasure in the mere possession of it. Helmut Thielicke warns that we theologians can all too easily succumb to the psychology of the possessor, the will to possess. And its fruit is rotten—a perverse joy that is quite unlike the joy of Christ, and a desire to take and boast that is quite the opposite of love and humility.[22] The antidote is maturing into Christ-normed childlikeness, as it produces the holy deference to grasp that doctrine

21. Dorothy L. Sayers, *Gaudy Night* (New York: Harper & Row, 1964), 465.
22. Helmut Thielicke, *A Little Exercise for Young Theologians*, trans. Charles L. Taylor (1962; repr., Grand Rapids: Eerdmans, 1998), 16–17.

is not entrusted to us, but we are entrusted to doctrine; that we do not determine the gospel, but the gospel determines us; that we do not make the Christian faith, but the faith makes us; that we do not speak, act, or know in our own name, but in the name of Father, Son, and Spirit. Theological formation of this sort stakes an absolute claim on us, as we are transformed by our trusting, loving participation in the reality of which theology speaks: God in Jesus Christ. But just as theology is no substitute for God, it has no independent reality, truth, or power apart from the God to whom it refers. When theology is pursued within an egocentric framework of one's own terms and ends—with the will to possess—it is reduced to collecting and cataloging items of information, making for a knowledge that is abstract, arbitrary, and insignificant. Free from the childlike deference that may cause us to blush, we are free to be lonely, unaffected, and bored.[23]

To be childlike as Christ is childlike is to unabashedly cherish being children of the Father. For our childlikeness is patterned after Christ's, the result of our union with him. We are thus loved with— indeed, included in—the love of the Father for the Son, an eternal love that is never fickle and never fails, a strong and sure love that is always gentle but never soft, a perfect love that teaches us that to fear the Lord is to need never be afraid of him. The name most precious to Jesus—Abba, Father—has been placed in our hearts and on our lips; the Spirit that Jesus bears without measure bears witness within us that, in the Son, we too are children of the Father; and as children, we have an inheritance kept for us—namely, to be heirs with Christ of all that the Father has (John 16:15; Rom. 8:15–17; Gal. 4:4–7; 1 Pet. 1:4). No wonder Scripture exclaims, "What no eye has seen, nor ear heard, nor the heart of man imagined, what God has prepared for those who love him" (1 Cor. 2:9). So as we inhabit the eschatological tension of the now and not-yet, moving toward a day when all that

23. Andrew Purves, *Reconstructing Pastoral Theology: A Christological Foundation* (Louisville: Westminster John Knox, 2004), xvi, 13–16; Marc Barnes, "Click Fix," *First Things* 263 (May 2016): 19–21. Barnes's work is a superb little piece about the camera-phone and therapeutic photography, but it has rich theological implications.

eludes even our loftiest imaginings is fully and finally realized, our heavenly Father treats us as who we truly are: beloved children. And for just this reason, he does perfectly throughout the entirety of our lives what all truly loving earthly parents do imperfectly and temporarily. Our Father disciplines the children he dearly loves:

> It is for discipline that you have to endure. God is treating you as sons. For what son is there whom his father does not discipline? If you are left without discipline, in which all have participated, then you are illegitimate children and not sons. Besides this, we have had earthly fathers who disciplined us and we respected them. Shall we not much more be subject to the Father of spirits and live? For they disciplined us for a short time as it seemed best to them, but he disciplines us for our good, that we may share in his holiness. For the moment all discipline seems painful rather than pleasant, but later it yields the peaceful fruit of righteousness to those who have been trained by it. (Heb. 12:7–11)

Discipline does not often disclose its benefits immediately, reminding us that life must be lived forward but can only be understood backward. Yet all the while we may be sure that, unlike mere childishness, Christ-normed childlikeness is not something we grow out of but is something we progressively grow into as our Father trains *all* his beloved children for what awaits them. The epistle to the Hebrews tells us that even Jesus "learned obedience through what he suffered" (Heb. 5:8). Does this imply that Jesus was ever *dis*obedient, that he ever sinned in thought, word, or deed? No. This same epistle teaches that Jesus faced every manner of trial, test, and temptation, all without sin (Heb. 4:15; cf. John 8:46; 1 Pet. 2:22; 1 John 3:5). Jesus learning obedience tells us that, from manger to cross, he experienced firsthand what it means to trust and love the Father under the conditions of human existence east of Eden. Our Lord was not born glorified. Rather, he was glorified after flawlessly obeying the Father against the ever-stiffening headwinds of human and diabolical opposition that he faced all the way to Golgotha. The life he lived qualified him for the death he died, rendering him a spotless Savior and sympathetic high priest (Heb. 2:10; 4:15; 1 Pet. 1:19). And the Father disciplines us so that we may mature into the childlikeness that results from being forged and fashioned in Christ's image. Our theological formation occurs east of Eden as well, amid many of the trials, tests, and temptations that Jesus faced and bested, and against opposition from the world that is both human and devilish. Here, then, our good Father lovingly disciplines us so that our understanding of reality might be tested, corrected, and enlarged, so that the deep and bracing things of God might make us people of the truth, people of theological wisdom and fortitude, resilience and discernment. If we are to mature toward the measure and stature of Christ, we must put away childish things—not least the desire to be very grown up—and become truly childlike indeed.

In the World, Not of the World

Jesus Christ calls Christians to bear confident, competent witness to the world, and theology is essential to our mission. Theology helps the church bless the world, not least because theology helps us rightly distinguish the church from the world, knowing where and how she differs. To this end, we must grasp that when Jesus speaks of the "world" (Greek, *kosmos*), he rarely means the universe or planet Earth in general. Most often he means the domain of darkness, death, and the devil, the sum of sinful humanity marked by self-lordship and God-defiance (John 3:19–20; 7:7; 14:30; 15:18–19; 16:8–11; cf. Eph. 2:1–3). It is precisely *this* world in rebellion and revolt against God that he so fiercely loves, the world for which the Father gave his only-begotten Son, and for which the Son gave himself unto death (John 3:16; Rom. 5:6–8). Just as the Father sent Jesus into the world, Jesus sends us into the world, to manifest the truth and self-giving love that marks children of the Father. Jesus sanctifies us in the truth and leads us into the world for the life of the world, to love the world in the same way and with the same redemptive aim as God loves the world.

Christians are called to share Christ's mission *in* the world because we, like him, are not *of* the world. We are not superior to the world, nor does God seek to insulate and isolate us from it. Rather, our Lord chose us out of the world to situate us in the world as his own, freeing us from the allegiances, agendas, and ideologies of the world so that we are free to be his disciples (John 17:14–19). We are to love the world that Christ loved all the way to Golgotha. And because he is the love and truth of God incarnate, we must see as myths all notions of truthless love or loveless truth. In Jesus Christ, love is the substance of truth, and truth is the shape of love. Consequently, loving the world in the truth of the God who is love means not loving many things that the world loves; it means not loving the world on its own terms, toward its own ends; it means not reducing God's holy love to the unholy indulgence, sentimentality, and omni-affirmation that all too often masquerades as love in modernity. This is the sense in which the apostle John cautions: "Do not love the world or the things in the world. If anyone loves the world, the love of the Father is not in him. For all that is in the world—the desires of the flesh and the desires of the eyes and pride of life—is not from the Father but is from the world. And the world is passing away along with its desires, but whoever does the will of God abides forever" (1 John 2:15–17).

Jesus Christ is not of the world, because he is from the Father, come to bring life to a world that futilely seeks life in itself. The tension of the now and not-yet compels Christians to inhabit the world as those who are likewise not of the world, but from the Father in Christ. Raised with the Risen One, we are an eschatological people, the new humanity burgeoning forth amid an old and weary world that is even now passing away. We are not misplaced persons—stuck, stranded, and seeking merely to endure our regrettable stay. Neither are we tourists—carefree, uninvolved sightseers on a breezy excursion. We are resident aliens, for whom the world can never be trivial or ultimate, but instead, the sphere where we have been divinely placed for missional investment and action. The paradox of our present existence is thus to resist the world yet not retreat from it, to be concerned for the world yet not be conformed to it, to live peaceably with all people so far as is possible yet not settle for that hollow peace the world offers at the price of infidelity to our Lord (Rom. 12:2, 18). We are not to be ill-natured misanthropes but magnanimous contrarians, intent on the world's benefit but under no illusion that the world is benign. For our nail-pierced Savior bears wounds that prove otherwise, and he tells us plainly and repeatedly that the world loves its own, not Christ's own (John 15:18–19; 16:33; 17:14; cf. 2 Tim. 3:12). D. A. Carson explains: "The world is a society of rebels, and therefore finds it hard to tolerate those who are in joyful allegiance to the king to whom all loyalty is due. . . . Those who preach Jesus' gospel and live in progressive conformity to his own life and teaching will attract the same antagonism that he did."[24]

Any world where Christians need not take up and put on the whole armor of God is simply not the world described by Jesus and the apostles. It is a mythical world, an unreal world, out of step and out of sorts with the one *Christ-reality*. Yet this is crucial: we do not ultimately contend with people, but with the powers of this present darkness, the spirit of the age, the forces of evil at work in the world (Eph. 6:10–20). And the central point of contention is none other than Jesus Christ himself. He is the light who lays bare the darkness of the world, a mission of truth and love to those lost in the darkness, so they might come to know him as their true salvation and only real hope (Matt. 10:34–39; John 3:16–21). However, the world does not contend with CEO Jesus, therapist Jesus, political activist Jesus, personal success coach Jesus, nature mystic Jesus, or any such notion of our Savior. These are at home in the world because they are of the world, idols cast in the world's own image and conscripted to its own agendas. No, the world contends with the Jesus who is God's image, come to do the Father's will—the Jesus of Scripture, King of kings and Lord of lords.

---

24. D. A. Carson, *The Gospel according to John*, Pillar New Testament Commentary (Grand Rapids: Eerdmans, 1991), 525.

The difference between Christians and the world is theological at its core and to its depths, since the point of contention—the watershed, the great divide—is the Christ who *is* our theology, our *Theos-Logos*, the God-Word. Here, then, theology offers both the church and the world alike an invaluable gift: forthright truth in love about the life-and-death difference between them. For Christians can thrive in the world only when we are rooted with well-formed resolve in the true vine who is Christ, only when we have theological facility in the faith we are called to cherish, uphold, and warmly commend to the world. Our only actual alternative to theological formation is thus a theological naivete that invites either resignation and withdrawal from the world or capitulation and assimilation to it, a dereliction of discipleship that could only leave us clueless, defenseless, and useless—the epitome of insipid salt and shrouded light. Further, it is only when we can ably and unambiguously bring the gospel to bear on the world that those yet of the world can repent and receive the gospel's God—or at very least, that they can be offended for all the right reasons, granted haunting lucidity about the Christ they persist in rejecting.[25]

Jesus Christ is the difference between Christians and the world, and in him the church is an eschatological body whose head is the King of an eschatological kingdom. Jesus has established his kingdom in the world, and its advance affects the world, but this kingdom is neither sourced by nor subservient to the world (John 18:36–37). This means that Christians seeking relevance on the world's terms travel the shortest and surest route to irrelevance. For we become relevant to the world by being responsive to the kingdom, making our most significant and distinctive contribution in the now by living forward into the reality of the not-yet. And Christ's kingdom is not an abstraction, an impersonal thing, a desired end to which our Lord is but the means. Just as Jesus is the incarnate Way, Truth, and Life of God, divine wisdom, righteousness, and holiness embodied, so too is he the

25. Victor Shepherd, *Our Evangelical Faith* (Toronto: Clements, 2006), 72.

presence of the kingdom in person. Before anything else we confess about the kingdom, then, let us grasp that Christ is its substance and sum, its reality and aim. As Origen rightly declares, Jesus Christ is the "absolute Kingdom," or the *autobasileia*, the kingdom in himself.[26]

Christ-ian theology is theology for the eschatological tension of the now and not-yet, as it is oriented to and ordered by the kingdom of Christ in person. Therefore, it helps us resist the siren song that would make us culturally trendy according to the world instead of prophetically timely according to the kingdom, that idolatrous snare that would have us see Christ not as a matchless end in himself but as a means to still greater and grander personal or social goals. Here political ideologies are among the most powerful and seductive forces presently at work in our politically preoccupied world. For these are often religious, but not that of Jesus, making thinly veiled ploys to fill the God-shaped vacuum of our secular age by conscripting us to other lords, converting us to other gospels, and committing us to other kingdoms that promise unity and meaning not from above but from below—not from the Father according to the Spirit of Christ but from the world according to the spirit of the age.

If Christ's kingdom were of the world, his people might do well to be preoccupied with the politics of the world. But because Christ's kingdom is *not* of the world, all such preoccupations are divisive and disorienting blights on our baptismal identity and the church's witness in the world. Clear-eyed and stout-hearted theological discernment is the antidote to this malady that mistakes and exchanges Christ's kingdom for "leftist" or "rightist" sociopolitical outlooks on the world. Our Lord's kingdom is equidistant from both, and all others beside, *qualitatively* different from every vision for the world

---

26. Origen, *Commentary on the Gospel of Matthew* 14.7, in *ANF*, 9:498. Origen's observation about the kingdom applies quite readily to any attempt to abstract Christ's benefits from Christ himself, to sunder gift from Giver. In the words of Michael Reeves, "The center, the cornerstone, the jewel in the crown of Christianity is not an idea, a system or a thing; it is not even 'the gospel' as such. It is Jesus Christ." *Rejoicing in Christ* (Downers Grove, IL: IVP Academic, 2015), 10.

that does not begin and end with his kingly act and address. This does not make Christians apolitical or loath to render unto Caesar what is Caesar's. Rather, it allows us to be truly political. In allegiance to our King as kingdom citizens we are free to love our neighbors in the truth, free to seek kingdom righteousness amid this passing world in eager anticipation of that coming world without end. Indeed, the church must not do otherwise, since the King of the kingdom is the Lord of all creation, making us a peculiar people, called to herald the gospel in word and deed as public truth for all peoples. As Eberhard Busch observes, "The decisive point here is that the church can speak and act politically *only* as *church*, only in its hearing of the Word of God and only in his service."[27] C. S. Lewis punctuates this point via his fictional demon Screwtape, who counsels his tempter in training on the diabolical art of helping Christians confuse and conflate the gospel of Christ's kingdom with the gospels of the world:

> Certainly we do not want men to allow their Christianity to flow over into their political life, for the establishment of anything like a really just society would be a major disaster. On the other hand we do want, and want very much, to make men treat Christianity as a means; preferably, of course, as a means to their own advancement, but, failing that, as a means to anything—even to social justice. The thing to do is to get a man at first to value social justice as a thing which the Enemy [God] demands, and then work him on to the stage at which he values Christianity because it may produce social justice.[28]

The church speaks with integrity and vitality in the world only as she hears the living voice of Christ in Scripture; thus the church must speak and steward the language of Scripture, which is the language of theology. Christians have long confessed, and wisely so, that the rule of prayer is the rule of faith—that how we pray shapes what

---

27. Eberhard Busch, *The Barmen Theses Then and Now*, trans. Darrell Guder and Judith Guder (Grand Rapids: Eerdmans, 2010), 75 (emphasis original).
28. C. S. Lewis, *The Screwtape Letters* (New York: HarperCollins, 2001), 126–27.

we believe. Yet we must likewise grasp with the same strength of conviction that the rule of speech is the rule of thought—that how we speak shapes what we think. There is a relationship of reciprocal reinforcement between speaking and thinking, and the world knows this well. That is why many of the institutions and influencers of our age are busily leading a rapid, top-down revision of language around several key topics: sex, gender, marriage, ethnicity, diversity, equality, justice, and the like. And that is why these same powers attempt to regulate the discourse around these topics with all the religious zeal we might expect from a most scrupulous and exacting catechist: *because catechesis is the intent*. Theology is our first line of defense against patterns of speaking and thinking that would conform us to the world, because theology safeguards Christian language from being shorn of Christian content, so that our words can continue to orient us to reality—to Christ and his kingdom. Theology allows ongoing fidelity of speech and thought, so we can say and think true things about the way things truly are, lest the church's understanding be reduced to basically that of the world with merely a thin, clichéd veneer of "Christian" verbiage. Our call is to remain fiercely yet humbly undaunted as we speak the truth in love, not tossed or spun about by the doctrines of the world's orthodoxy that cunningly hide new, strange content behind old, familiar words (Eph. 4:14–15).[29] Alexander Schmemann is spot-on:

> The discernment of spirits . . . is above all a differentiation of words, for not only did the word, with the world and all creation, fall, but the fall of the world began precisely with the perversion of the word. Through the word entered that lie whose father is the devil. The poison of this lie consists in the fact that the word itself remained the same, so that when man speaks of "God," "unity," "faith," "piety," "love," he is convinced that he knows of what he is speaking, whereas

---

29. Dietrich Bonhoeffer, "Becoming Real Theologians," in *The Trials of Theology: Becoming a "Proven Worker" in a Dangerous Business*, ed. Andrew J. B. Cameron and Brian S. Rosner (Fearn, Ross-shire, UK: Christian Focus, 2010), 73–74.

the fall of the word lies precisely in that it inwardly became "other," became a lie about its own proper meaning and content. The devil did not create new, "evil" words, just as he did not and could not create another world, just as he did not and could not create anything. The whole falsehood and the whole power of this falsehood lie in the fact that he made the *same* words into words *about something else*, he usurped them and converted them into an instrument of evil and that, consequently, he and his servants in "this world" always speak in a language literally stolen from God.[30]

Jesus situates his church in the world to be first and foremost a worshiping community, and the church worships with integrity and vitality when that worship radiates her deep rootedness in *Christian* theology. For this worship manifests the church's conformity to Christ—the ultimate theologian and worshiper—and so it also manifests that the church is not of the world. Yet our Lord differentiates us from the world so that we may be rightly in and for the world, so that we may make disciples of all nations, teaching all that Jesus commands and baptizing in the triune name of Father, Son, and Spirit (Matt. 28:19–20). Truly Christian existence in the world is thus attended by Scripture and sacrament suffused with the Spirit-wrought power of Christ's abiding presence, showing forth that we are crucified to this world, risen with Christ, and partakers even now in the firstfruits of the world to come. This worship declares that our orientation is toward the kingdom of our King, that our identity and destiny are determined by the Christ who is in and for the world but not of it, that ours is the triune God of the gospel, who rids us of all would-be gods and gospels. Indeed, worship rooted in *Christ-ian* theology exudes the aroma of Christ, so it is to the world what Christ is to the world: the grandest of blessings and the gravest of threats, a sweet fragrance to those being saved and a foul stench to those

30. Alexander Schmemann, *The Eucharist: Sacrament of the Kingdom*, trans. Paul Kachur (Crestwood, NY: St. Vladimir's Seminary Press, 1987), 148 (emphasis original).

holding fast to sin and death, a provisional no that gives way to the profoundest yes for all with open ears, open hearts, and open hands (2 Cor. 2:14–17; 4:1–6). Jean-Jacques von Allmen poignantly states:

> Every time the Church assembles . . . to "proclaim the death of Christ" (1 Cor. 11:26), it proclaims also the end of the world and the failure of the world. It contradicts the world's claim to provide men with a valid justification for their existence, it renounces the world: it affirms, since it is made up of the baptized, that it is only on the other side of death to this world that life can assume its meaning. . . . Christian worship is the strongest denial that can be hurled in face of the world's claim to provide men with an effective and sufficient justification of their life. There is no more emphatic protest against the pride and the despair of the world than that implied in Church worship.[31]

Pride and despair are equally and utterly groundless in the presence of Jesus Christ, because just as pride is confronted by the cross, despair is consoled by the empty tomb. But while we are even now partakers in new and eternal life, present participants in Christ's dying and rising, we await another resurrection—the full and final redemption of our bodies in the age to come. So our Christian life is lived like our Christian theology is done: between two resurrections and two advents, amid the eschatological tension of the now and not-yet. As we inhabit and embrace this tension we learn to live forward and understand backward, to mature into childlikeness, to be in the world but not of the world—all in response to God's glorious devastation of human life and history by the miracle of grace. To apprehend the one *Christ-reality* is thus to see with a bifocal vision that is world affirming and world denying, and is emphatically both at once. That is why the church has shown prodigious industry and creativity in art, music, and literature; in building and operating schools, colleges, hospitals, and orphanages; in caring for the poor

---

31. Jean-Jacques von Allmen, *Worship: Its Theology and Practice* (London: Lutterworth, 1966), 63.

and oppressed; and in pursuing manifold reforms and advances in human rights. At the same time, that is why Christians must remain vigilant—indeed, altogether insistent—that our share in Christ's mission to the world is never made to advance any other vision of the kingdom than that of our King.[32] Let us treasure in our hearts and ponder longingly the words of Lesslie Newbigin:

> The point is that [a transformed society] is not our goal, great as that is. . . . Our goal is the holy city, the New Jerusalem, a perfect fellowship in which God reigns in every heart, and His children rejoice together in His love and joy. To that we look forward with sure hope, and for its sake we offer up to God all that we do in response to His invitation to love our neighbor as we ourselves have been loved. And though we know that we must grow old and die, that our labors, even if they succeed for a time, will in the end be buried in the dust of time, and that along with the painfully won achievements of goodness, there are mounting seemingly irresistible forces of evil, yet we are not dismayed. We do not need to take refuge in any comfortable illusions. We know that these things must be. But we know that as surely as Christ was raised from the dead, so surely shall there be a new heaven and a new earth wherein dwells righteousness.[33]

---

32. Os Guinness, *Prophetic Untimeliness: A Challenge to the Idol of Relevance* (Grand Rapids: Baker Books, 2003), 49–50.

33. Lesslie Newbigin, *Signs Amid the Rubble: The Purposes of God in Human History*, ed. Geoffrey Wainwright (Grand Rapids: Eerdmans, 2003), 55.

Conclusion

Six Theses on the Character
of Christian Theology

We began this book with wise words from J. I. Packer, who insisted that knowledge of God is the greatest and grandest goal of human existence: "What aim should we set ourselves in life? To know God. . . . What is the best thing in life, bringing more joy, delight and contentment than anything else? Knowledge of God. . . . What, of all the states God ever sees man in, gives God most pleasure? Knowledge of himself."[1] Joy, delight, contentment, pleasure: these sorts of words best describe the character of theology. For theology is about knowing the God who exudes joy, brings true delight, grants everlasting contentment, and is, to be sure, eminently pleasurable. B. B. Warfield, legendary professor of theology at Princeton Seminary (1887–1921) and lifelong student of theology himself, lovingly exhorted his students about their task at hand:

> I am here today to warn you to take seriously your theological study, not merely as a duty, done for God's sake and therefore made divine,

1. J. I. Packer, *Knowing God*, 20th anniv. ed. (Downers Grove, IL: InterVarsity, 1993), 33.

but as a religious exercise, itself charged with religious blessing to you; as fitted by its very nature to fill all your mind and heart and soul and life with divine thoughts and feelings and aspirations and achievements. You will never prosper in your religious life in the Theological Seminary until your work in the Theological Seminary becomes itself to you a religious exercise *out of which you draw every day enlargement of heart, elevation of spirit, and adoring delight in your Maker and your Savior.*[2]

Warfield's counsel is fitting for every last student of theology—young or old, just getting started or well along the way, pastor, college or seminary student, and anyone else besides. For all of us, the goal of theology is the same: to know and love God with all our heart, soul, and mind. So standing atop the shoulders of Packer and Warfield, as it were, and indeed the whole holy host of our beloved forebears in the faith, we offer the following six theses on the character and calling of theology.

1. Theology involves accepting the call from our Lord Jesus Christ to have the whole of us transformed by the whole of him, so as to be conformed to the one Christ-reality of God. Jesus has a gift to give us, and it is sublime. It is the gift of sharing in his mind; the gift of participating in his love and knowledge of the Father; the gift of understanding and experiencing the world as he created and redeemed it. Through union with Christ in his death and resurrection and in Spirit-vivified acquaintance with Scripture, our Lord reorients us to reality, granting us to think, speak, and act in the world according to its divine design. Because Jesus is the Truth of God, the Truth of humanity, and the Truth of the world, he liberates us in himself to be a people of the Truth: "If you abide in my word, you are truly my disciples, and you will know the truth, and the truth will set you free" (John 8:31–32).

---

2. Benjamin B. Warfield, "The Religious Life of Theological Students," in *Selected Shorter Writings of Benjamin B. Warfield*, ed. John E. Meeter (Nutley, NJ: Presbyterian and Reformed, 1970), 417 (emphasis added).

2. *Theology is captivated by and preoccupied with the triune God of the gospel.* When Jesus calls us to love God with our heart, soul, and mind, his aim is to usher us into a life-giving, life-transforming, reality-altering relationship with his Father in the power and presence of the Spirit. Because God neither is nor ever shall be other than the Holy Trinity that he always has been, we can only think and speak about God, and only worship God, *as* Holy Trinity. And that is impossible—yes, impossible—unless by an act of sheer grace God the Son causes us to know God the Father in the communion of God the Spirit. The apostle Paul's benediction is thus perfectly fitting for grasping the character of theology: "The grace of the Lord Jesus Christ and the love of God and the fellowship of the Holy Spirit be with you all" (2 Cor. 13:14).

3. *Theology serves the life, worship, and mission of the church.* While lectern and lecture can be enormously fruitful contexts for doing theology, it is primarily in pulpit and proclamation that the true character of theology is enacted. It is in the heralding of God's Word and the reception of God's promises in water, bread, and wine that God's people come to know and experience God. All faithful, fruitful theology derives its meaning from theology's native and natural habitat in the church, where the body and bride of Christ hears, proclaims, prays, sings, and imbibes the Word of God. Therefore, all truly *Christ-ian* theology, whether done in lecture hall or living room, has its origin in the gathering of the saints, and its end in fortifying the saints in their mission to the world. Theology exists to help the church delight in the triune God. And if theology does not serve that grand goal of glorifying God and enjoying him forever, then it is, quite simply, not worth doing.

4. *Theology is a way of life.* Theology expresses the deepest truths of our lives, because it expresses the Truth of God, in whom alone we have life. As such, living theologically is not an *option* for Christians; it is the way we allow the gospel to saturate, suffuse, and shape our lives from one day to the next. To reiterate Tish Harrison Warren's observation, "If I am to spend my whole life being transformed by the good news of Jesus, I must learn how grand, sweeping truths—doctrine, theology, ecclesiology, Christology—rub against the texture of an average day. How I spend this ordinary day in Christ is how I will spend my Christian life."[3] Her words express the ancient wisdom of the church, that our lives are lived—day to day, year to year, season to season—in accord with how God has revealed himself in Christ. To live theologically is thus to live liturgically, to spend the moments of our lives in the knowledge that the Jesus of Scripture has become for us the meaning and measure of a new and redeemed time.

5. *Theology always originates in divine revelation.* Because the subject of theology is the living, speaking God of Scripture, theology is beholden to his active voice. Theology thus recognizes that what is truly rational is what is truly revelational. To be sure, the exercise of human reason is utterly indispensable for theological formation. Yet the truly wise theologian learns that human reason must always bow in glad submission to the mysterious voice of God in order to be truly rational. Kelly Kapic observes that this is the difference between foolishness and wisdom: "The foolish person lives as though individuals can decide whether or not God exists, and if he does exist, what God's activities can be like. . . . The wise person recognizes the limits of human reason and perception and therefore delights in the fact that the eternal One has unveiled himself and has invited us to know and abide with him."[4] Theology is an exercise in knowing and abiding with God, such that his wisdom might make us foolish people wise.

6. *Theology requires and produces holy humility.* The call to Christian formation is a call to know the God whose thoughts and ways transcend our own. Precisely because the *truth* of God is the truth of *God*, that truth cannot be exhausted or domesticated by us. Therefore, theology cheerfully understands that while our knowledge

3. Tish Harrison Warren, *Liturgy of the Ordinary: Sacred Practices in Everyday Life* (Downers Grove, IL: InterVarsity, 2016), 24.
4. Kelly M. Kapic, *A Little Book for New Theologians: Why and How to Study Theology* (Downers Grove, IL: IVP Academic, 2012), 27.

of God is wholly sufficient, it is of yet incomplete. What now is in the presence of the Word made flesh and what is yet to come in his coming again call us to inhabit a God-ordained tension, the eschatological tension in which all theology is done this side of glory. For the God we know truly and really in Christ is the God we know in part and dimly (1 Cor. 13:12). *Christ-ian* theology thus grasps that in the now and not-yet we must mature into childlikeness as we seek to live in the world but not of the world by the cruciform strength of our crucified Lord. All the while, theology teaches us to listen so that we might learn to hear, and to hear so that we might learn to think, speak, and act. Helmut Thielicke is correct: "If we are to have serious dealings with God it is essential that we be quiet and first of all do nothing but simply listen and let ourselves be questioned. When we do, we shall make the astonishing discovery that Christianity is not, as we supposed, an answer to our questions. . . . On the contrary, it is Christianity that asks the serious questions and therefore teaches us what true questioning is."[5]

It is time for the holy body and bride of Christ to retrieve her theological voice, to regain her wholehearted, full-throated witness to the gloriously good news of the gospel. Indeed, the church faces myriad cultural, ideological, and sociopolitical headwinds that seek to stifle and stymie that witness. May our Lord call forth resolute hope, making these headwinds the occasion for a revival of theology that directs us to the reality of God and makes sense of our world. It is often said, and rightly so, that every Christian is a theologian. Then may our seeking to be good and faithful Christians entail our striving to be good and faithful theologians.

---

5. Helmut Thielicke, *Out of the Depths*, trans. G. W. Bromiley (Grand Rapids: Eerdmans, 1962), 55.

Scripture Index

Subject Index